50 WALKS IN THE
Yorkshire Dales

50 Walks in the Yorkshire Dales

Published by AA Publishing (a trading name of AA Media Limited, whose registered office is Grove House, Lutyens Close, Lychpit, Basingstoke, Hampshire RG24 8AG; registered number 06112600)

© AA Media Limited 2023
Fifth edition
First edition published 2002

Mapping in this book is derived from the following products:
OS Landranger 91 (walk 1)
OS Landranger 92 (walks 2, 4)
OS Landranger 97 (walks 10, 13)
OS Landranger 98 (walks 3, 6-9, 11-12, 14-16, 22-27)
OS Landranger 99 (walks 5, 17-21, 28)
OS Landranger 103 (walks 29-30, 33, 43, 47-49)
OS Landranger 104 (walks 31-32, 34, 36, 38-42, 44-45)
OS Landranger 105 (walk 37)
OS Explorer 21 (walk 46)
OS Explorer 288 (walk 50)
OS Explorer 297 (walk 35)

© Crown copyright and database rights 2023 Ordnance Survey. 100021153.

Maps contain data available from openstreetmap.org © under the Open Database License found at opendatacommons.org

ISBN: 978-0-7495-8330-9
ISBN: 978-0-7495-8356-9 (SS)

A CIP catalogue record for this book is available from the British Library.

AA Media would like to thank the following contributors in the preparation of this guide:
Clare Ashton, Tracey Freestone, Lauren Havelock, Nicky Hillenbrand, Ian Little, Richard Marchi, Nigel Phillips and Victoria Samways.

Cover design by berkshire design company.

We would like to thank the following photographers, companies and picture libraries for their assistance in the preparation of this book. Abbreviations for the picture credits are as follows:
Alamy = Alamy Stock Photo
Trade cover: Andrew Hopkins/Alamy
Special sales cover: PSC-Photography/Alamy
Back cover advert clockwise from bottom left: courtesy of The Plough, Lupton; SolStock/iStock; AA; EmirMemedovski/iStock
Inside: 12/13 Andrew Kearton/Alamy; 29 Clearview/Alamy; 39 richard sowersby/Alamy; 55 Seriousreindeer/Alamy; 71 John Blackburn/Alamy; 93 andy aughey/Alamy; 112-113 Anyka/Alamy; 123 Mark Sunderland/Alamy; 130-131 LEE BEEL/Alamy; 147 Ros Crosland/Alamy; 163 Bailey-Cooper Photography/Alamy

Printed by Stamperia Artistica Nazionale - Trofarello - TORINO - Italy

A05836

AA

50 WALKS IN THE
Yorkshire Dales

CONTENTS

The walks

HOW TO USE THIS BOOK

Each walk starts with an information panel giving all the information you will need about the walk at a glance, including its relative difficulty, distance and total amount of ascent. Difficulty levels and gradients are as follows:

Difficulty of walk

● Easy

● Intermediate

● Hard

Gradient

▲ Some slopes

▲▲ Some steep slopes

▲▲▲ Several very steep slopes

Maps

Every walk has its own route map. We also suggest a relevant Ordnance Survey map to take with you, allowing you to view the area in more detail. The time suggested is the minimum for reasonably fit walkers and doesn't allow for stops.

Route map legend

‒ ‒ ‒ ‒	Walk route	▢	Built-up area
❶	Route waypoint	▢	Woodland area
‒ ‒ ‒ ‒	Adjoining path	🚻	Toilet
•	Place of interest	P	Car park
⌂	Steep section	🎪	Picnic area
⋇	Viewpoint	)(	Bridge
⠿⠿⠿	Embankment		

Start points

The start of each walk is given as a six-figure grid reference prefixed by two letters referring to a 100km square of the National Grid. More information on grid references can be found on most OS Walker's Maps.

Dogs

We have tried to give dog owners useful advice about how dog friendly each walk is. Please respect other countryside users. Keep your dog under control, especially around livestock, and obey local bylaws and other dog control notices.

Car parking

Many of the car parks suggested are public, but occasionally you may have to park on the roadside or in a lay-by. Please be considerate about where you leave your car, ensuring that you are not on private property or access roads, and that gates are not blocked and other vehicles can pass safely.

Walks locator map

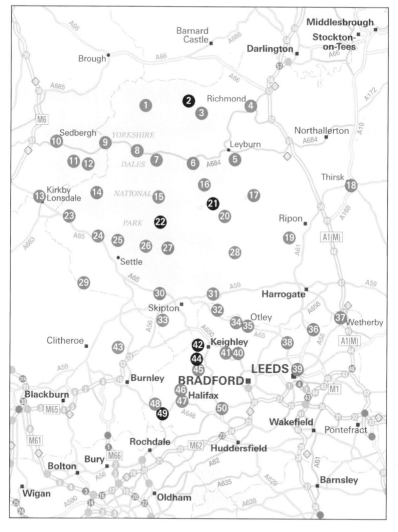

EXPLORING THE AREA

The Yorkshire Dales are a series of beautiful valleys spreading out from the high Pennine watershed to the north of the industrial heartlands of West Yorkshire. For the most part they are protected by the Yorkshire Dales National Park, which covers an area of some 684 square miles (1,773sq km) across the upland centre of northern England. Dominated by gritstone and limestone, the Dales attract thousands of visitors every year.

SWALEDALE

In the north, Swaledale is the most peaceful and least developed of these valleys. It was once a centre for lead mining and knitting, but now tourists bring most of its income, attracted by the remote villages such as Reeth, Keld and Muker, and the breathtaking contrasts of light and dark, meadows and brooding hills. Richmond and its great castle guard the entrance to the dale, where the River Swale spills into the Plain of York. In the tributary valley of Arkengarthdale, the landscape is scarred by lead mining, the abandoned workings adding a fascinating historical dimension to walks here.

WENSLEYDALE

Next is Wensleydale, famous for its crumbly cheese and ceaseless waterfalls, of which Aysgarth and Hardraw are the highlights. The scenery is less bleak than its northern neighbour, with larger villages like Bainbridge and Hawes serving as pretty honeypots. The map says this is Cumbria, but the scenery is still Yorkshire Dales at heart.

RIBBLESDALE

Still on the western side, Ingleton and Settle are the centres for exploring the limestone uplands that drain into the Ribble and Lune. You may stray into Lancashire here, perhaps to the shapely summit of Pendle Hill or the fringes of the Forest of Bowland which lines the west of Ribblesdale. Here, too, you'll find the Devil's Bridge at Kirkby Lonsdale, a soaring medieval structure over the River Lune, with the dark heights of Barbon Fell a brooding backdrop.

WHARFEDALE

Wharfedale, with its origins high on the fells at Oughtershaw, cuts a curving U-shaped line between craggy tops and limestone side valleys, past Hubberholme, Kettlewell and Grassington, then the ruins of the priory at Bolton Abbey. From here the scenery changes subtly, the valley widening between heather moorlands through elegant Ilkley and, after one last moorland flourish on Otley's Chevin, beyond into the plains. From the ancient stone circle near the top of Ilkley's famous moor you can see for over 50 miles (80km), perhaps picking out the Kilburn White Horse on the North York Moors or the tower of York Minster on a clear day.

NIDDERDALE

Beside the Wharfe runs Nidderdale, a quiet, unassuming valley with great reservoirs in its upper reaches. Left out of the Yorkshire Dales National Park, this tranquil corner of grouse moors, pastureland and scattered settlements is now protected by the Nidderdale Area of Outstanding Natural Beauty.

AIREDALE

Running parallel with the Wharfe is the River Aire. It cuts through gentle countryside to the fringes of West Yorkshire. Here it narrows and the distinctive dark stone is shaped into mills and workers' houses. Above them brood silent moors, where the Brontë sisters found their inspiration. Most of the mills have long ceased production and in Bingley and Haworth the industrial past blends into a picturesque present of tumbling becks and woods bedecked with spring bluebells.

CALDERDALE

Calderdale winds down from the bleak moors above Todmorden through villages and towns once dominated by textile mills, but now softened and healed by time. The sheltered little wooded cloughs that line the main valley were once full of industry, but now you can forget how close you are to the heart of urban West Yorkshire.

LEGACY

Across this landscape strode giants, poets, great writers and storytellers. But it is usually the humble workers we have to thank for the exhilarating opportunities to explore the region on foot. Miners trod their paths up the gills and beneath the crags to find lead and coal. Drovers ushered their cattle and sheep down the dales and over the fellsides on their way to the southern markets. Strings of ponies carried freight over passes and bridges to keep more populous regions in salt and wool. Mill workers hurried down stepped and paved tracks to work in the mill. This is the real legacy of the Dales, and their best kept secret.

PUBLIC TRANSPORT

Where the Dales run into Metropolitan West Yorkshire, the public transport network is coordinated by Metro. It is relatively cheap, trains and buses run into the evening, and day passes are available. Find out more at www.wymetro.com, or call MetroLine on 0113 245 7676. In more rural areas and the Yorkshire Dales National Park, public transport is less plentiful and times more inconvenient. However, there are frequent buses in summer from some towns to popular walking areas. Get timetable information at www.dalesbus.org. Arriva Northern operates trains on the Settle-to-Carlisle line. For more information call the National Rail enquiry line on 03457 48 49 50, or check www.nationalrail.co.uk.

WALKING IN SAFETY

All these walks are suitable for any reasonably fit person, but less experienced walkers should try the easier walks first. Route-finding is usually straightforward, but you will find that an Ordnance Survey walking map is a useful addition to the route maps and descriptions; recommendations can be found in the information panels.

Risks

Although each walk here has been researched with a view to minimising the risks to the walkers who follow its route, no walk in the countryside can be considered to be completely free from risk. Walking in the outdoors will always require a degree of common sense and judgement to ensure that it is as safe as possible.

- Be particularly careful on cliff paths and in upland terrain, where the consequences of a slip can be very serious.

- Remember to check tidal conditions before walking on the seashore.

- Some sections of route are by, or cross, busy roads. Take care, and remember that traffic is a danger even on minor country lanes.

- Be careful around farmyard machinery and livestock, especially if you have children with you.

- Be aware of the consequences of changes in the weather, and check the forecast before you set out. Carry spare clothing and a torch if you are walking in the winter months. Remember that the weather can change very quickly at any time of the year, and in moorland and heathland areas, mist and fog can make route-finding much harder. Don't set out in these conditions unless you are confident of your navigation skills in poor visibility.

- In summer remember to take account of the heat and sun; wear a hat and carry water.

- On walks away from centres of population you should carry a whistle and survival bag. If you do have an accident that means you require help from the emergency services, make a note of your position as accurately as possible and dial 999.

Countryside Code
Respect other people:

- Consider the local community and other people enjoying the outdoors.

- Co-operate with people at work in the countryside. For example, keep out of the way when farm animals are being gathered or moved, and follow directions from the farmer.

- Don't block gateways, driveways or other paths with your vehicle.
- Leave gates and property as you find them, and follow paths unless wider access is available, such as on open country or registered common land (known as 'open access land').
- Leave machinery and farm animals alone – don't interfere with animals, even if you think they're in distress. Try to alert the farmer instead.
- Use gates, stiles or gaps in field boundaries if you can – climbing over walls, hedges and fences can damage them and increase the risk of farm animals escaping.
- Our heritage matters to all of us – be careful not to disturb ruins and historic sites.

Protect the natural environment:
- Take your litter home. Litter and leftover food don't just spoil the beauty of the countryside; they can be dangerous to wildlife and farm animals. Dropping litter and dumping rubbish are criminal offences.
- Leave no trace of your visit, and take special care not to damage, destroy or remove features such as rocks, plants and trees.
- Keep dogs under effective control, making sure it is not a danger or nuisance to farm animals, horses, wildlife or other people.
- If cattle or horses chase you and your dog, it is safer to let your dog off the lead – don't risk getting hurt by trying to protect it. Your dog will be much safer if you let it run away from a farm animal in these circumstances, and so will you.
- Everyone knows how unpleasant dog mess is and it can cause infections, so always clean up after your dog and get rid of the mess responsibly – bag it and bin it.
- Fires can be as devastating to wildlife and habitats as they are to people and property – so be careful with naked flames and cigarettes at any time of the year.

Enjoy the outdoors:
- Plan ahead and be prepared for natural hazards, changes in weather and other events.
- Wild animals, farm animals and horses can behave unpredictably if you get too close, especially if they're with their young – so give them plenty of space.
- Follow advice and local signs.

For more information visit www.gov.uk/government/publications/the-countryside-code

3. Bear left down a walled track, signed 'Muker'. After a gate the track becomes metalled, finally descending through two gates into a walled lane on the edge of the village. Continue to a T-junction.

4. Turn left and in a few paces left again by a sign to Gunnerside and Keld. Follow the paved path through six gates to the river. Turn sharp right, signed 'Gunnerside', and walk downstream to a footbridge.

5. Ascend steps beyond the footbridge and turn left, signed 'Keld'. Follow a clear track up along the valley, until it curves right into Swinner Gill. Cross a footbridge by the remains of lead workings, and go up to a wooden gate.

6. Go straight ahead up the hill to another gate and on through woodland. The track levels out, then it starts to descend, winding left round a barn then swinging back right. Continue steadily downhill through a gate to reach a gate above East Gill Force.

7. Fork left by a wooden seat, at a Pennine Way sign. Follow the path down to a footbridge, cross it, then bear right, uphill, to a T-junction, where you turn right and follow the track back to the car park.

Where to eat and drink

Muker has a top-notch tea room, attached to the Village Store. The Farmers Arms, just behind the Village Store, provides excellent beer, plus good home-made bar meals in the cosy bar with its open fire. Park Lodge in Keld offers hot and cold drinks and snacks.

What to see

Around Muker traditional hay meadows are still to be found. They are an important part of the farmer's regime, which is why signs ask you to keep to single file as you walk through them. Such a method of farming helps maintain the wide variety of wild flowers that grow in the hay meadows. The barns, too, are part of older farming patterns, and form one of the most important visual assets of the Dales. The Muker area is especially rich in them – there are 60 such barns within 0.5 miles (800m) of the village. Their purpose was to store the hay after it was cut, to feed the three or four animals who would be over-wintered inside. This was to save the farmer moving stock and hauling loads of hay over long distances. It also meant that the manure from the cattle could be used on the field just outside the barn.

While you're there

Take the minor road that leaves the B6270 west of Keld to reach Tan Hill and its inn, the highest pub in England at 1,732 feet (528m) above sea level. With no neighbouring dwelling for at least 4 miles (6.4km) in any direction, it is as welcome a sight for walkers today as it was for the packhorse-train drivers of the past, and the coal and lead miners who worked on the surrounding moors. It's not advisable to attempt the drive in fog, snow or icy weather.

AROUND ARKENGARTHDALE

DISTANCE/TIME	8.5 miles (13.7km) / 3hrs 45min
ASCENT/GRADIENT	1,977ft (603m) / ▲
PATHS	Mostly clear tracks, some heather moor, 4 stiles
LANDSCAPE	Mining-scarred moorland, with evocative remains of industry
SUGGESTED MAP	OS Explorer OL30 Yorkshire Dales - Northern & Central Areas
START/FINISH	Grid reference: NZ005024
DOG FRIENDLINESS	Off lead for much of walk, except where sheep are present
PARKING	Pay-and-display car park at south end of Langthwaite village
PUBLIC TOILETS	Langthwaite

The quiet villages of Arkle Town and Langthwaite are grey clusters of houses in the austere splendour of Arkengarthdale. One of the most northerly of the valleys in the Dales, it runs northwards from Swaledale into dark moorland, with the battle-scarred Stainmore beyond its head. This isolation and stillness is deceptive, however, for until the beginning of the 20th century the surrounding hills were mined for lead. It was first dug here in prehistoric times, but industrial mining of the great veins of lead really began in the 17th century. By 1628 there was a smelt mill beside the Slei Gill, which you will pass on the walk, and there is still evidence of the early miners' methods.

Booze and gunpowder

Booze (Norse for 'the house on the curved hillside') is now just a cluster of farm buildings, but was once a thriving mining community with more than 40 houses. Between Booze and Slei Gill you will pass the arched entrance to a level (a miners' tunnel) and behind it the remains of Tanner Rake Hush. This desolate valley is full of tumbled rock, left when the dammed stream at the top of the valley was allowed to rush down, exposing the lead veins. You'll pass the spoil heaps of Windegg Mines, before returning to the valley near Scar House, now a shooting lodge owned by the Duke of Norfolk but once belonging to the mine master. Near Eskeleth Bridge is the powder house, a small octagonal building, set safely by itself in a field. Built about 1804, it served the Octagon Smelt Mill. Lord of the Manor Charles Bathurst held the mining rights in the 18th century and The CB Inn near the road junction is named in his honour.

Mining the west of the valley was more difficult than on the eastern side. This was an area known in the 19th century as the Hungry Hushes – the lead mined here was scarce and hard-won. The miners' tracks ascend the hill and eventually pass the junction of two long chimney flues. The walk then returns via Turf Moor into Langthwaite – it needs a feat of the imagination to visualise its heyday, with a tight-knit community of hardened miners and their families.

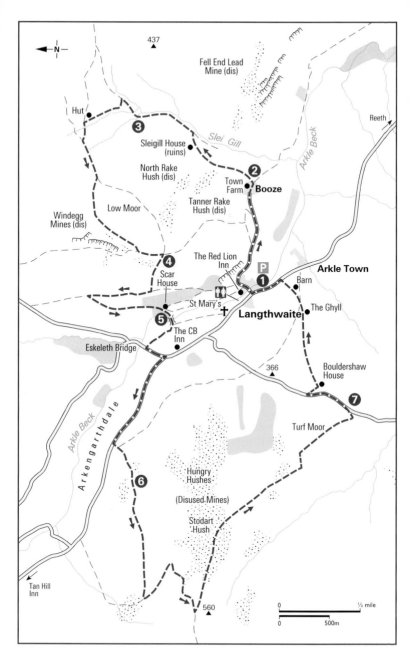

1. Leave the car park, turn right, then right over the bridge into Langthwaite. Climb the narrow lane between cottages. The lane becomes a track. Ignore two left forks and continue to the hamlet of Booze. Go straight through the yard of Town Farm and follow a rutted track up and left to a gate.

2. Continue ahead on a green track slanting down through spoil heaps and past ruined Sleigill House to the stream. Walk up the valley, go through a gate and cross the stream near a limekiln.

3. Climb the steep bank, go through new tree-plantings and follow green paths through the heather. Pass a wooden hut and turn left onto a broad track. Follow the main track through a slight but long valley, then bear left over the moor and down to a T-junction with a wall just below. Where this falls back, go down right to a gate in the corner.

4. Follow the small gully downhill and past waymarkers to a level track. Turn right and follow the track, traversing the hillside until it bends sharp left to meet a stony track. Turn left to a house then bear right, through the garden and down a slanting green track, eventually entering woodland.

5. Emerge alongside Scar House. Follow the drive downhill and over a bridge. Bear right on a walled track, then turn right through gateposts and walk to a road. Turn left, uphill, to a T-junction. Turn right and follow the road for 0.5 miles (800m). Opposite a barn, turn left on an obvious track.

6. Turn right at the far side of a gravelled area, then cross a grassy area and slant uphill towards a prominent flat-topped spoil heap. Just before this, the track bends sharp left then winds uphill to reach a T-junction near the crest. Turn left and follow the clear track, continuing along the ridge then bearing right down to a road.

7. Turn left. Pass above a farm (Bouldershaw), then turn right at a bridleway sign. Turn left just before the farmyard and go straight down a green track. At The Ghyll, join its access track but as it bends right bear left instead and down to a stile in the bottom right corner of the field. Go down to the road then turn left back to the car park.

Where to eat and drink

The Red Lion Inn in Langthwaite has good beer and lunchtime bar food. The CB Inn further up the road is more upmarket, with a noted restaurant serving fine, fresh food – best to book for evening meals.

What to see

Dry-stone walls are a typical feature of Arkengarthdale, as in much of the Yorkshire Dales. There are around 4,680 miles (7,530km) of such walls in the National Park, many of them built during the enclosure of former common land in the 17th to 19th centuries. These are the walls that head straight as an arrow for the fell tops. Earlier walls tend to enclose smaller fields and were built from rocks gathered from the fields – some may date from before 1000 BC. They provide shelter for sheep and for smaller animals and birds, such as whinchats. Many walls are derelict, and there are grants from various bodies available to farmers who want to repair them – but a lack of skilled wallers is slowing down these repairs.

While you're there

Continue up the road towards the head of Arkengarthdale and on to the 16th-century Tan Hill Inn, the highest pub in Britain at 1,732 feet (528m). Winters can last for six months here and ice 4in (10cm) thick has been known to form on the windows. The inn has hosted an annual sheep show on the last Thursday of May since 1951.

AROUND REETH IN THE HEART OF SWALEDALE

DISTANCE/TIME	5.5 miles (8.8km) / 2hrs
ASCENT/GRADIENT	612ft (187m) / ▲ ▲
PATHS	Field and riverside paths, lanes and woodland, 14 stiles
LANDSCAPE	Junction of Swaledale and Arkengarthdale, with fields and surrounding moorland
SUGGESTED MAP	OS Explorer OL30 Yorkshire Dales - Northern & Central Areas
START/FINISH	Grid reference: SE039993
DOG FRIENDLINESS	Dogs should be on leads for majority of walk
PARKING	In Reeth, by the Green (voluntary payment requested)
PUBLIC TOILETS	In Reeth, opposite the Buck Hotel and in Grinton

Reeth has always had a strategic role in the Yorkshire Dales. Set above the junction of Swaledale and Arkengarthdale on Mount Calva, it controlled the important route westwards from Richmond. Sheep were for a long time the basis of Reeth's prosperity – it has been a market town since 1695 – and there are still annual sheep sales each autumn, as well as the important Reeth Show around the beginning of September. The wool was used in Reeth's knitting industry – both the men and women would click away with their needles at stockings and other garments. Reeth also used to be a centre for the lead mining industry, which extended up Arkengarthdale and over Marrick Moor.

Two bridges and a church

Reeth Bridge, reached via the Leyburn road from the Green, has suffered over the years from the effects of the swollen River Swale. The present bridge dates from the early 18th century, replacing one washed away in 1701, itself built after its predecessor succumbed in 1547. The path beside the river leads to Grinton Bridge. Nearby is Grinton Church, once the centre of a huge parish that took in the whole of Swaledale, making very long journeys necessary for marriages and funerals. Curiously, it began life as a mission church for the Augustinian canons of far-away Bridlington Priory on the east coast.

Nuns and schools at Marrick

The approach to Marrick Priory along the lane suggests that you are about to reach one of the most important churches in the Dales. In a way, that is true. Marrick in the Middle Ages was home to a group of Benedictine nuns. It was founded by Roger de Aske, whose descendent, Robert, was a leader of the Pilgrimage of Grace, the uprising against King Henry VIII's closure of the monasteries. Hilda Prescott's novel *The Man on a Donkey* (1952), about Robert Aske and the pilgrimage, is partly set at Marrick. Today the nuns' buildings are partly demolished or absorbed into farm buildings. The church was reduced in size in 1811, and Marrick Priory is now an outdoor education and residential centre. After Marrick Priory the path climbs steeply uphill on rough stone steps called the Nun's Causey (a corruption of 'causeway'). Now used as part of the Coast to Coast Walk, from St Bee's Head in Cumbria to Robin Hood's Bay on the east coast, it is said to be built by the nuns from the priory. The original 365 steps have been broken up and removed over the centuries, but the path still retains a suitably medieval feel.

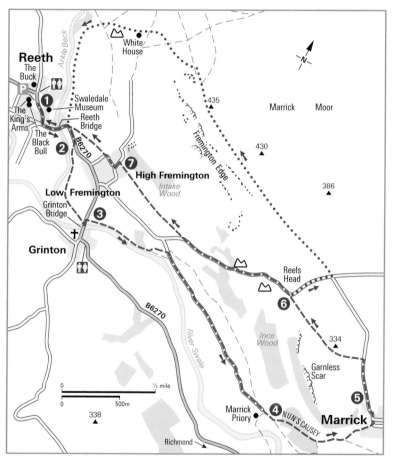

1. From the Green, walk downhill in the direction of Leyburn to Reeth Bridge. Over the bridge, continue along the road as it swings right. About 100yds (91m) along, turn right at a footpath sign to Grinton.

2. Follow the riverside path to a signpost, then continue on a well-marked path across fields to ascend steps onto Grinton Bridge. Turn left for a few paces, cross the road and take a track beside the bridge.

3. Follow the riverside path for about 0.5 miles (800m) to a metalled lane. Turn right and follow the lane to Marrick Priory. Walk past the buildings, over a cattle grid, and bear left through a gate signed 'Marrick'.

4. Walk up the grassy track, then follow the paved path through woodland. Continue through fields, with a wall on the right, into a metalled lane. Opposite Harlands House turn left, then left again at a triangular junction.

5. Follow the road for 0.25 miles (400m), and turn left over a stile at a footpath sign. Follow the wall and cross a waymarked stile. Continue along the wall, then keep on in the same direction, ascending slightly to meet a road.

6. Turn left and follow the road for 0.75 miles (1.2km). On a left bend near an obvious track to a farm, cross a stile on the right, signed 'Fremington'. Go straight ahead to a stile, then continue along the well-marked path through fields, until a final gate leads onto a walled path behind houses. Go straight ahead to a lane.

7. Turn left then first right. As the lane bends left, go ahead to a stile by a gate. Keep by the wall on the left, and follow the path through more stiles back to Reeth Bridge. Cross the bridge and follow the road back to the Green.

Extending the walk You can extend the walk from Point 6 by turning right, uphill, then left through a stile by the road sign to Marrick. Cross a field, follow a wall on the left, then keep on the track over Fremington Edge. Descend past spoil heaps, go through a gate and follow a faint path half right. Bear right along the brink of a very steep slope (beware the broken crags below), then slant down to a gap in a wall. Continue the slanting descent through the remains of chert mines. Reach a track near a footpath sign, follow a grassy path above White House to a gated stile, bear left on a green path and descend steeply to a track, signpost and stile. Cross the stile, walk past a barn and through two more stiles, then bear left, parallel with the river, with a wall on your left. Go through a stile, pass a barn, then go through the left of two gates in a crossing wall. Continue through a long narrow field to the road by Reeth Bridge, rejoining the main walk.

Where to eat and drink
The King's Arms and the Black Bull (next door to each other) and The Buck in Reeth all provide good food at lunchtime and in the evenings. There are also tea rooms and cafés around the Green.

What to see
Swaledale sheep are a hardy breed. They are equipped for their life on exposed moorland with thick wool that is very resistant to water. When spun it is very hardwearing, and modern treatment methods remove any harshness.

While you're there
The little Swaledale Museum in Reeth has displays about life in the Dales, including lead mining, knitting, farming and stone-walling as well as original historic photographs of the Dales.

RICHMOND AND EASBY ABBEY

DISTANCE/TIME	6.5 miles (10.4km) / 2hrs 45min
ASCENT/GRADIENT	1,318ft (402m) / ▲▲
PATHS	Field and riverside paths, some town walking, 15 stiles
LANDSCAPE	Valley of River Swale and its steep banks
SUGGESTED MAP	OS Explorer 304 Darlington & Richmond
START/FINISH	Grid reference: NZ168012
DOG FRIENDLINESS	Dogs should be on leads for most of walk
PARKING	Nunns Close long-stay car park
PUBLIC TOILETS	Nuns Close car park in Richmond town centre and Round Howe car park

The first part of the walk follows much of the route taken by the legendary Richmond drummer boy. At the end of the 18th century, the story says, soldiers in Richmond Castle discovered a tunnel that was thought to lead from there to Easby Abbey. They sent their drummer boy down it, beating his drum so they could follow from above ground. His route went under the Market Square and along to Frenchgate, then beside the river towards the abbey. At the spot now marked by the Drummer Boy Stone, the drumming stopped and the boy was never seen again. The Green Howards Regimental Museum in the Market Square can tell you more about the drummer boy and his regiment.

Abbey and church

Easby Abbey, whose remains are seen on this walk, was founded for Premonstratensian Canons in 1155 by the Constable of Richmond Castle. Although not much of the church remains, some of the other buildings survive, including the gatehouse, built about 1300. The refectory is also impressive, and you can see the infirmary, the chapter house and the dormitory.

Just by the abbey ruins is the parish church, St Agatha's. It contains a replica of the Anglo-Saxon Easby Cross (the original is in the British Museum) and a set of medieval wall paintings showing Old Testament scenes of Adam and Eve on the north wall, and the life of Jesus on the south, as well as depictions of activities such as pruning and hawking. After the abbey, you'll cross the River Swale on the old railway bridge and follow the trackbed. This was part of the branch line from Richmond to Darlington, which opened in 1846 and closed in 1970. The station has been restored as a cinema and shopping centre, with a café. Look right over Richmond Bridge after you have passed below the castle to see how the stonework differs from one end to the other. It was built by different contractors, one working for Richmond Council and one for the North Riding of Yorkshire. In the hillside below Billy Bank Wood, which you enter beyond the bridge, were copper mines dating back to the 15th century.

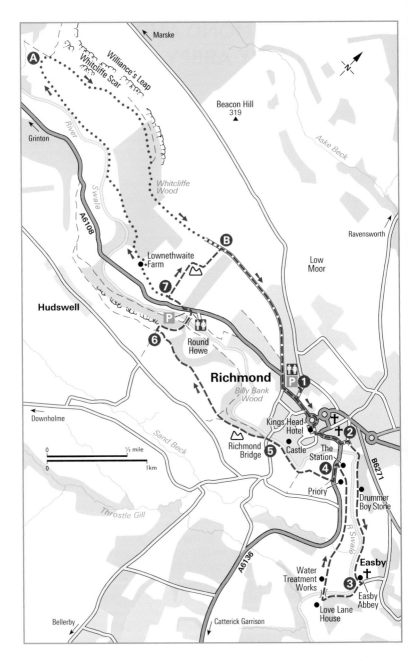

1. Leave the car park and turn right, then left at the T-junction onto Victoria Road. At the roundabout go straight on down Ryder's Wynd. At the bottom turn left, then go right into Station Road. Just past the church, take Lombards Wynd left.

2. Turn right at the next junction and follow the track, passing to the right of the Drummer Boy Stone, along the path to a gate. Bear right after the gate, still parallel with the river, bearing right again to a gate, then along beside the abbey in the village of Easby.

3. Just beyond the car park turn right along the track. Follow the wall on the left to Love Lane House. Turn right over the old railway bridge. Follow the trackbed, crossing a metalled lane, to the station. Go to the left of the station building to the road.

4. Turn left up the road, then turn right up Priory Villas, bearing right to go in front of the houses. Go through three waymarked gates, keeping parallel to the river. Cross some playing fields and pass a clubhouse to a road.

5. Cross the road and take a signed path opposite, to the left of the cottage. Climb steeply through the woodland, through a gate and straight on to a stile. At the end of the woodland, bend right, then left to pass a stile in a former crossing fence. Follow the signed path over 12 more stiles. After the last, bear right over another stile, turn left to follow the wall, then go over another stile.

6. Turn right to go through a gate. Follow the track as it bends downhill, through a gate, to a bridge. Cross it and walk to the lane. Go left and left again at the main road. After 200yds (183m), go right up a bridleway-signed track to a junction.

7. Turn right and follow the track uphill, bearing right, then left near the farmhouse, to reach a metalled lane. Turn right and follow the lane back into Richmond. Go ahead at the main road and follow it as it bends left to the garage, where you turn left back to the car park.

Extending the walk You can extend this walk by continuing up the banks of the River Swale, along the tracks from Point 7, as far as Point A. Return beneath the crags of Whitcliffe Scar to rejoin the main route at Point B.

Where to eat and drink
The Kings Head Hotel in the Market Square in Richmond has meals, sandwiches and afternoon teas. The café in The Station is a popular meeting place, and is well-known for its cakes.

What to see
Wynds (from the Old English word for 'to spiral') are narrow lanes usually linking two wider streets. You'll see Friar's Wynd to your right, beside the Georgian Theatre Royal, as you begin the walk, and you'll go down Ryder's Wynd and along Lombard's Wynd. This last was once part of the ancient route up from the banks of the River Swale to the northeastern area of the town around Frenchgate – 'Frankesgate' in the Middle Ages.

While you're there
Visit Richmond Castle, which looms over the Swale Valley through much of the walk. Its keep, more than 100ft (30m) high, was complete by 1180. The castle's central ward is surrounded by high curtain walls with towers. Inside the keep are unique drawings made in World War I by conscientious objectors.

EXPLORING MIDDLEHAM AND ITS CASTLE

DISTANCE/TIME	7 miles (11.3km) / 2hrs 30min
ASCENT/GRADIENT	475ft (145m) / ▲
PATHS	Field paths and tracks, with some road walking, 13 stiles
LANDSCAPE	Gentle farmland, riverside paths, views of Wensleydale
SUGGESTED MAP	OS Explorer OL30 Yorkshire Dales – Northern & Central Areas
START/FINISH	Grid reference: SE127877
DOG FRIENDLINESS	Livestock and horses in fields, so dogs on leads
PARKING	In square in centre of Middleham
PUBLIC TOILETS	Middleham

When Richard III died at the battle of Bosworth Field in 1485, Middleham lost one of its favourite residents. He had lived here – in the household of the Earl of Warwick, 'The Kingmaker' – when a boy, and then with the Earl's daughter Anne after their marriage. As Duke of Gloucester, it was his power base as effective ruler of the North under his brother Edward IV. Locals don't believe the propagandist version of Richard, promoted by Shakespeare's play, that he was a murderer – the Lord Mayor of York reported after Bosworth that 'King Richard, late lawfully reigning over us, was through great treason piteously slain and murdered'.

Middleham Castle today is a splendid ruin, with one of the biggest keeps in England, impressive curtain walls and a deep moat. From Middleham, the walk takes you to the River Cover and along its banks. After crossing Hullo Bridge the path passes near Braithwaite Hall. Owned by the National Trust and open by appointment only, this is a modest 1667 farmhouse, with three fine gables and unusual oval windows beneath them. On the hillside behind are the earthworks of a hill-fort, thought to be Iron Age.

The lane eventually crosses Coverham Bridge, probably built by the monks of nearby Coverham Abbey. There are a few remains of the abbey, mostly incorporated into later buildings on the site. Miles Coverdale, who was the first man to complete a full English translation of the Bible, came from here.

Middleham

For many people, Middleham is the home of famous racehorses, and you may be lucky enough to see some training as you walk over Middleham Low Moor towards the end of the walk – make sure you keep out of their way. Both the Low Moor and the High Moor have been used for exercise for more than 300 years. Among early jockeys was the splendidly named 'Crying Jackie' Mangle, who won the St Leger five times in the 1770s and 1780s. To your left as you leave the Low Moor and make your way back to the castle is William's Hill, the remains of the original motte-and-bailey castle built here by the Normans after 1066 to guard the approaches to Wensleydale and Coverdale. The motte, 40ft (12m) high, is joined by a curved bailey surrounded by a ditch. It was abandoned in 1170 when the new castle was begun nearby.

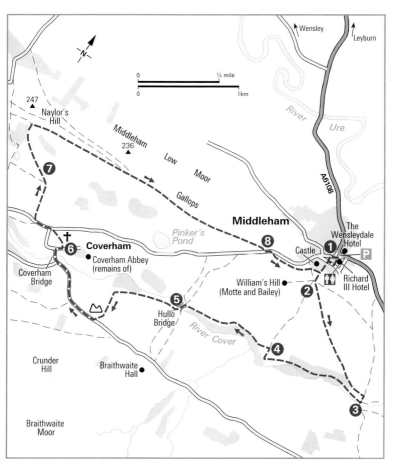

1. From the square take Coverham Lane, then turn left up a passage beside the Castle Keep Tea Room. Continue left of Middleham Castle along a walled track to a gate.

2. Bear left across the big field, following the sign for 'stepping stones' to the field corner. Go over a stile and cross two more fields, over waymarked stiles. After the third stile, follow the field-edge above a steep bank. At a crossing wall turn right, down to the River Cover by the stepping stones.

3. Turn right (do not cross the river) and follow the path through woods and a narrow field. Bend right at the end to a gate and continue to steps and an elevated section. After returning to the river bank, cross a stile into a field. Bear half right across the field to an ascending track.

4. Follow the track, which becomes a path and follows fenced woodland on your left. Continue to a stile on your left, go through a narrow band of woodland to a second stile, then straight ahead on an obvious descending path. Cross a stile and turn left to Hullo Bridge.

5. Cross the gated bridge and turn right on a permissive path, crossing two stiles. At a crossing wire fence turn left. Cross another stile. Where the fence bends right, go ahead onto a track and bear right to reach a gate onto a lane. Turn right and descend to Coverham Bridge. Cross the bridge and turn right on a track.

6. Before iron gates, turn left through a small gate, climbing beside a waterfall into the churchyard. Bear left to leave by the lychgate and bear left along the main road (signed to Forbidden Corner). Where the wide grass verge on the right ends, turn right at a footpath signed 'Tipgill'. Walk between gateposts and up the track. At the top, go through a gate and bear half left to go through two more gates through a belt of woodland.

7. Then head half right across the field to go through a gate below a house. Follow the fence to your left, uphill, to bend left beyond the house to a gate onto a track. Turn right, go through gateposts and turn right again on a wide track. Where the track bends right, keep straight ahead across the grassy moor; look for occasional blue-topped posts marking the line of a bridleway. When the long fenced gallops appear, keep them to your left and continue down to a gate onto the road.

8. Turn left and, just before the Middleham sign, take a signposted path on the right. Cross the gated stile, turn left and follow the path that is parallel to the road. Go through a stile and four gates onto the lane, then turn left and return to the square.

Where to eat and drink
Middleham's Wensleydale Hotel and adjoining Tack Room serves from 10am–6pm Wednesday to Sunday. The Richard III Hotel has a varied bar menu. The Castle Keep is a good, friendly tea room.

What to see
If you're lucky, you may see the iridescent blue and orange of a kingfisher above the waters of the River Cover. Vulnerable to pollution and harsh winters, kingfishers live in the banks of the river, digging a burrow up to 3ft (1m) deep and constructing a nest for six or seven eggs. Kingfishers catch fish with their fearsome bills and carry them back to their perches. They turn them so the head faces outwards, and stun them against the perch before swallowing them whole.

While you're there
Nearby Wensley, after which the dale takes its name, was once a market town, but plague in 1563 reduced it to a little village. Visit the church to see the monumental brass to the priest Simon de Wensley – one of the best in the country – and the wonderful Scrope family pew, partly made of the rood screen from Easby Abbey near Richmond.

6

FROM WEST BURTON TO AYSGARTH

DISTANCE/TIME	4 miles (6.4km) / 2hrs
ASCENT/GRADIENT	394ft (120m) / ▲
PATHS	Field and riverside paths and tracks, 40 (mostly squeeze) stiles
LANDSCAPE	Two typical Dales villages, fields and falls on the River Ure
SUGGESTED MAP	OS Explorer OL30 Yorkshire Dales - Northern & Central Areas
START/FINISH	Grid reference: SE017867
DOG FRIENDLINESS	Dogs should be on leads
PARKING	Centre of West Burton, by (but not on) the Green
PUBLIC TOILETS	None on route; Aysgarth National Park visitor centre is close

Many people regard West Burton as the prettiest village in the Dales. Its wide, irregular green, with a fat obelisk from 1820, is surrounded by stone cottages, formerly homes to quarrymen and miners – but there's no church. West Burton has always been an important centre, at the entrance to Bishopdale, with its road link to Wharfedale. South is the road to Walden Head, now a dead end for motorists, but for walkers another route to Starbotton and Kettlewell.

Two halves of Aysgarth

After crossing the wide flood plain of Bishopdale Beck, and Eshington Bridge, you climb across the hill to descend into Aysgarth. A village of two halves, the larger part, which you come to first, is set along the main road. The walk takes you along the traditional field path to the other half, set around St Andrew's Church. It's worth looking inside at the spectacular choir screen. Like the elaborate stall beside it, it was carved by the renowned Ripon workshops.

The falls and the wood

The path follows the river beside Aysgarth's Middle and Lower Falls, formed by the Ure eating away at the underlying limestone as it descends from Upper Wensleydale to join the deeper Bishopdale. They are now one of the most popular tourist sights in the Yorkshire Dales National Park.

Mrs Sykes' follies

On the return leg of the walk you pass below two follies in the parkland behind the house at Sorrelsykes Park. They were built in the 18th century by a Mrs Sykes. One is a round tower, with a narrowing waist like a diabolo. The other, sitting like Thunderbird 3 ready for lift-off, is known locally as the 'Rocket Ship'. It is of no practical use, except for minimal shelter in the square room in its base, but it is just one of many folly cones throughout Britain. None of the others, however, have this elaborate arrangement of fins – presumably the builder had doubts about its stability.

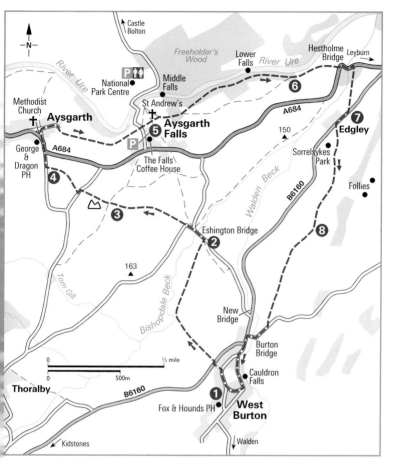

1. Leave the Green near the village shop. Opposite 'Meadow Croft' go left, signed 'Eshington Bridge'. Cross the road (B6160), turn right then left, to go through a gate and down steps. Go through a gate beside a barn, and continue to a stile at the bottom right of the field. Cross another stile, then bear right to meet a stone wall. Follow this, then continue over a stile in the same direction to reach a road.

2. Turn left, cross the bridge and go up a narrow lane to a bend. Go ahead through a stile, signed 'Aysgarth'. Climb through another stile and left of a barn. Continue through a gate up the field and bear left to a gate near the corner, then diagonally across the next field. Keep left of a wall gap to go through another gap by a small wood. Descend to a stile and footpath sign.

3. Continue in the same direction and up to a signpost. Follow the Aysgarth direction to a gateway and stile. Cross the field half left to a stile onto a lane. Turn left, then right, signed 'Aysgarth'. Go ahead through three stiles to a road.

4. Turn right into Aysgarth. Go past The George and Dragon then straight ahead to the Methodist church and bear right along the lane. Cross a stile by

Field House. Follow the wall to another stile and continue along a short track, then follow a path through eight stiles to a road.

5. Enter the churchyard, pass to the right of the church and leave by a stile. Cross a field and go through a wood over two stiles. Follow the path downhill, walking parallel with the river. Take a signed stile right.

6. Follow the path by the river over several stiles to a signpost. Bend right across a field to the main road (A684). Turn left, cross a bridge, then turn right into woodland, signed 'Edgley', soon bearing left uphill to a stile. Bear right across a field to a gate in the far corner and join a road (B6160).

7. Turn right. About 150yds (137m) along, go left over a stile, signed 'Flanders Hall'. Walk towards the follies, then bear right just below the ridge, passing Sorrelsykes Park to your right. Cross a track to a signpost, bear left up the bank, then follow the fence. Bear right to a stepped stone stile, then follow the bottom edge of the field to a gate opposite a stone barn.

8. Descend through this and two more gates, then bear left along the field edge to go over three stiles. Continue ahead to a lane. Turn right, cross a bridge and join the village road. Turn left, back to the Green.

Where to eat and drink

In Aysgarth, the George and Dragon is a good family pub serving meals. Up the road from the church is The Falls Coffee House, open Wednesday to Sunday 10am–3.30pm for home-cooked food. In West Burton, the Fox and Hounds is a traditional village pub serving meals. Aysgarth Falls National Park Centre, near Point 5, has a good coffee shop.

What to see

The woods around Aysgarth have long been used for the production of hazel poles. Now-overgrown stumps of hazel trees sprouting many branches, some of them of considerable age, are evidence of this trade. In Freeholders' Wood beside the Middle and Lower Falls, across the River Ure from the route of the walk, the National Park Authority has restarted this ancient craft of coppicing. Each year the hazel trees are cut back to a stump – called a stool – from which new shoots are allowed to grow. As long as they are protected from grazing cattle, the shoots develop into poles, and can be harvested after around seven years' growth. Hazel poles are traditionally used for making woven hurdles, and the thinner stems for basket-weaving.

While you're there

Get a sense of what a medieval castle was really like at Bolton Castle, in the village of Castle Bolton, 3 miles (4.8km) northeast of Aysgarth. Beneath its massive walls there are archery and falconry displays, a herb garden and vineyard, and a tea room, too – plenty to keep everyone occupied.

UP AND AROUND SEMERWATER

7

DISTANCE/TIME	5 miles (8km) / 2hrs 25min
ASCENT/GRADIENT	853ft (260m) / ▲ ▲
PATHS	Field paths and tracks, very steep ascent from Marsett, 18 stiles
LANDSCAPE	Valley, lake and fine views over Wensleydale
SUGGESTED MAP	OS Explorer OL30 Yorkshire Dales - Northern & Central Areas
START/FINISH	Grid reference: SD921875
DOG FRIENDLINESS	Dogs should be on leads
PARKING	Car park at north end of lake: fee payable at Low Bean Farm nearby
PUBLIC TOILETS	None on route

Semerwater was formed at the end of the last Ice Age. Glacial meltwater tried to drain down the valley the glacier had gouged out of the limestone, but was prevented by a wall of boulder clay dumped by the glacier across the valley's end. So the water built up, forming a lake which once stretched 3 miles (4.8km) up Raydale. Natural silting has filled the upper part of the lake bed, leaving Semerwater – at 0.5 miles (800m) long, North Yorkshire's largest natural lake.

Legendary Semerwater

Semerwater boasts several legends. One concerns the three huge blocks of limestone deposited by the departing glacier at the water's edge at the north end of the lake. Called the Carlow Stone and the Mermaid Stones, they are said to have landed here when the Devil and a giant who lived on Addlebrough, the prominent hill a mile (1.6km) to the east, began lobbing missiles at each other. More famous is the story of the beggar who came to the town that once stood where the lake is now. He went from door to door, asking for food and drink, but was refused by everyone except the poorest couple. Revealing himself as an angel, he raised his staff over the town, crying 'Semer Water rise, Semer Water sink, And swallow all save this little house, That gave me meat and drink.' The waters overwhelmed the town, leaving the poor people's cottage on the brink of the new lake. Some say the church bells can still be heard ringing beneath the waters.

Behind the legend

There are indeed the remains of a settlement beneath Semerwater. Houses on stilts perched along the water's edge in Iron Age times, though there may have been an earlier settlement here in neolithic times, too. Setts and Quakers Marsett, at the lake's southern end, and Countersett, to the north, both end with the Old Norse word denoting a place of hill pasture. Marsett is a hamlet of old farmhouses, and on the road to Countersett, at Carr End, is the house where Dr Fothergill was born in 1712. A Quaker philanthropist, he founded the Quaker school at Ackworth in South Yorkshire. Countersett has one of several old Friends' Meeting Houses in Wensleydale, and the hall was home, in the 17th century, to Richard Robinson, who was responsible for the spread of Quakerism in the Dales.

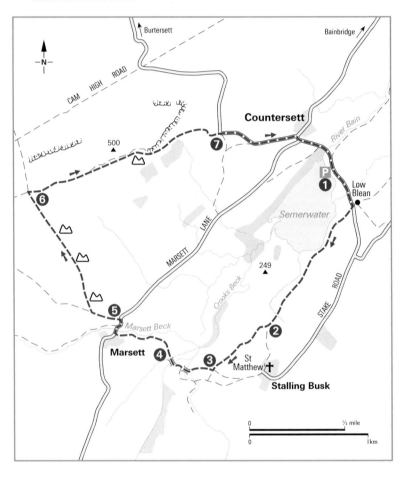

1. Turn right from the car park up the road. Opposite Low Blean farm go right over a ladder stile, signed 'Stalling Busk'. Cross another two stiles and continue towards a barn. Pass through a stile right of it to find a clearer path. Follow this, leaving the lake behind. Continue past an information board and then skirt above an old graveyard to a gate and signpost just beyond.

2. Follow the Marsett sign into the field corner and cross a gated stile. Take the level path through more stiles, then across a larger field, keeping just above a steeper slope. Pass right of a barn among trees, then cross a stream bed.

3. Bear right immediately on a narrow path, descending above a roofless barn to a stile. Continue over another stile to a stile at the corner of another barn, then turn right immediately across a level meadow, with a wall on your right. Cross the wall at a gate, then follow the path to a gated footbridge. Cross and go straight ahead to another footbridge beside a ford.

4. Continue along the obvious track through a gate, meeting another river. Approaching Marsett, bear right across a green, following the stream, to a red telephone box. Turn right over the bridge then after 100yds (91m) take a track signed 'Burtersett and Hawes' (not the path by the river).

5. Walk uphill to a gate on the right where the wire fence ends. Cross the stile and climb beside the wall up a faint but direct (and generally steep) path. Go over a stile and through a gate in a crossing fence. Reaching a ladder stile with an Access Land symbol, go straight ahead up a final steep slope, then more easily on a green path to a crossing track just below the final crest.

6. Turn right along the track to a gate on the skyline. Continue to a green knoll with views to the west. Descend to a gate, then follow the steep track downhill, winding below crags then slanting down the slope on a grooved track. Follow the track through three gates as it bends right and back left to reach a road.

7. Turn right and follow the road downhill to a staggered crossroads on the edge of Countersett. Turn right, then left, signed 'Stalling Busk'. Descend the lane over the bridge and back to the car park.

Where to eat and drink

The nearest place to Semerwater is Bainbridge, where the Rose and Crown Hotel dates back more than 500 years. The Bainbridge Horn, once blown to guide travellers to the village in the dark winter months, hangs here. The hotel serves home-cooked local produce in the bars and, in the evening, also in the Dales Room Restaurant.

What to see

Semerwater offers a wide variety of habitats for wildlife. The waters of the lake, which have a high plankton content, support many fish including bream and perch, as well as crayfish. Water birds include great crested grebe and tufted duck. You may also occasionally see whooper swans. Over the fringes of the lake, dragonflies and damsel flies can be seen glittering in the summer. On the wet margins of the lake grow flowers such as marsh marigold, marsh cinquefoil, ragged robin and valerian, while in the drier areas the wood anemone is frequently found. Birds such as lapwings, redshanks and reed buntings may also be seen, while summer visitors include the sandmartin.

While you're there

Visit Bainbridge, with its wide green and attractive houses. The Romans had a fort here, Virosidum, on top of the hill called Brough. The River Bain, crossed by the bridge which gives the village its name, is England's shortest river, running all of 2 miles (3.2km) from Semerwater to the River Ure.

8

DISCOVERING HAWES AND HARDRAW

DISTANCE/TIME	5 miles (8km) / 2hrs
ASCENT/GRADIENT	426ft (130m) / ▲
PATHS	Field and moorland paths, may be muddy, 35 stiles
LANDSCAPE	Moorland and farmland
SUGGESTED MAP	OS Explorer OL30 Yorkshire Dales - Northern & Central Areas
START/FINISH	Grid reference: SD870898
DOG FRIENDLINESS	Dogs under close control throughout; lots of stiles
PARKING	Pay-and-display car park off Gayle Lane at west side of Hawes
PUBLIC TOILETS	On Market Place, near car park

For many people, Hawes means two things – Wensleydale cheese and motorcyclists. The bikers use the town as a base on summer weekends and bank holidays, enjoying a friendly drink in the pubs and spectacular rides nearby. However, it is the Wensleydale Creamery that attracts other visitors. Near the car park in Gayle Lane, the Creamery offers tours, tastings and the chance to buy traditional Wensleydale cheese. Cheese has been made in Wensleydale since French monks brought the skill here in 1150. A factory was started in Hawes in 1897 and, after twice being saved from closure, it is now a thriving business and a vital part of the Hawes economy.

Force of nature

The walk gives you the chance – which you should take – to visit the famous Hardraw Force, a 90ft (27m) waterfall in a deep and narrow valley. Access to the waterfall is via the left of the Green Dragon Inn, then it's a short pleasant walk. Despite appearances, what you see isn't entirely natural. On 12 July 1889 an unprecedented deluge on the hill above caused a wall of water to descend Hardraw Beck and through the valley, destroying buildings in the village and washing away bridges. It also devastated the waterfall, reducing it to a mudslide. After seeing to the clearing up in the village and the welfare of his tenants, the local landowner, Lord Wharncliffe, arranged for his workmen to reconstruct the lip of the fall, pinning together the blocks of shattered stone. This he did so successfully that today's visitors have no idea of the disaster.

Bands in the valley

On the way to and from Hardraw Force you will pass the circular bandstand for the annual Hardraw Scar Brass Band Contest, usually held in September. It was founded in 1881, and is reputed to be the second oldest brass band competition in the world. Bands are cheered on by supporters who crowd the valley floor and hillsides of this natural amphitheatre.

Old ropes – and new

From the tiny village of Sedbusk, near the end of the walk, came the area's first-known rope maker, John Brenkley, who died in 1725. The tradition is continued today in Hawes by W R Outhwaite and Son at Hawes Ropeworks. Visitors can see work in progress on ropes for bells, barriers and banisters, as well as dog leads and braids.

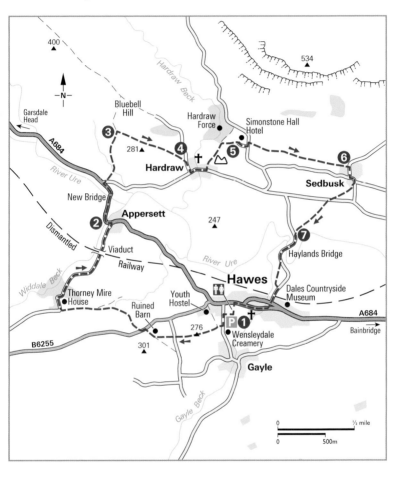

1. From the car park turn left. Just before the Creamery turn right between houses. Follow the left side of the field to a stile at the top. Keep straight on past a barn and across a lane. After passing a ruined barn, bear right to the B6255. Turn left, then right through a gate signed 'Thorney Mire House'. Follow the path, which bears left between parallel walls, for half a mile (800m) to meet a lane. Turn right and follow this to the A684 at Appersett.

2. Turn left over the bridge. Continue over another bridge to a junction, turn right and go straight over a stile, signed 'Bluebell Hill'. Bear slightly right to a gate and over a bridge, then bear left uphill to reach a gate. Continue past waymarkers to a signpost.

3. Turn right and walk to a stile (Bob's Stile) then bear slightly right to a prominent ladder stile. Walk straight ahead and Hardraw soon appears. Continue down over a stile, then over a ladder stile into a lane.

4. Turn right, then left at the main road. The entrance to Hardraw Force is just beside the Green Dragon Inn. Immediately after the pub, turn left, then right through a signed gap in the wall and through a courtyard. Follow a flagged path and steps uphill to a house. Turn right behind it, pass to the right of the stables, then bear slightly left to pass below the grounds of Simonstone Hall Hotel, joining its drive.

5. Walk down to a road and turn left. Almost immediately turn right through a stile signed 'Sedbusk'. Follow the track past farm buildings to a ladder stile, then continue straight ahead. Skirt below a house and continue over more stiles, along a flagged path and between houses into Sedbusk.

6. Turn right along the road, bend left near the postbox and descend. Go right, over a stile signed 'Haylands Bridge'. Cross the field, bear right below a wall-corner to a stile, then descend to a stile by the right end of a line of trees. Cross the lane to another stile and follow an obvious path across a stream. Descend to a humpback bridge and continue to a road.

7. Turn left and cross Haylands Bridge. About 200yds (183m) beyond, go right through a kissing gate signed 'Hawes'. Follow the path to a track, turn left a few paces, then right onto the main road. At the junction, carefully cross the first road, then turn right past the post office. Follow the main road through Hawes. Immediately before the public toilets, turn left up steps to the car park.

Where to eat and drink

There is plenty of choice in Hawes with its pubs, cafés and tea rooms, as well as a fish-and-chip shop. The Simonstone Hall Hotel, between Hardraw and Sedbusk, is upmarket but does offer meals and afternoon teas.

What to see

Redshank and widgeon are among the birds that you may see on the walk, especially around the pond by the New Bridge near Appersett (the second one you cross here). The wading redshank, with its long legs, has a characteristic alarm call and nests in grass, laying four eggs during the breeding season from April to July. Look out for the characteristic white bar across its wings. Widgeon, members of the duck family, graze on wet meadowland, often in huge flocks. The male has a rusty-red head with an orange crown, while the female is plainer, though of a distinctive dull orange colour.

While you're there

To find out more about life in the Dales, visit the Dales Countryside Museum in the Station Yard at Hawes. Here you can walk through a 'Time Tunnel' that takes you back through 10,000 years of Dales' history, to see how life has changed over the centuries. Also included in the admission charge is a trip 'down' a lead mine, a visit to an old doctor's surgery, and the nostalgia of a kitchen in the Dales from the last century.

A WALK THROUGH GRISEDALE

DISTANCE/TIME	5 miles (8km) / 2hrs 15min
ASCENT/GRADIENT	868ft (265m) / ▲
PATHS	Moorland paths and tracks, may be boggy, 16 stiles
LANDSCAPE	Rough moors and hidden valleys, railway within earshot
SUGGESTED MAP	OS Explorer OL19 Howgill Fells & Upper Eden Valley
START/FINISH	Grid reference: SD787918
DOG FRIENDLINESS	Sheep on moorland – keep dogs on leads
PARKING	Roadside parking on road to Garsdale Station
PUBLIC TOILETS	None on route

Grisedale is often tagged 'The Dale that Died'. This unfortunate label was the title of a television documentary made in the mid-1970s that followed the fortunes, and misfortunes, of families farming in this remote valley, which pushes north from Garsdale towards the massive heights of Wild Boar Fell. The programme dealt in particular with a former miner, Joe Gibson, who struggled against the climate, bad luck and the lack of subsidies for upland farmers, to try to make a living from the land – a struggle that eventually ended with his departure. The fields that Joe and his neighbours tended have now reverted to moorland and scrub, and a plantation of conifers climbs the side of East Baugh Fell from the valley bottom. Nearly all the farmhouses are derelict. At the head of the valley stands Round Ing, once a substantial building with barns and animal sheds. It has now fallen into disrepair but what remains of the plants and shrubs in its garden still bloom in summer.

From the pigs to the railway

Grisedale's earlier history is obscure – perhaps unsurprisingly for such a remote place. Its name comes from Old Norse and means 'the valley in which the pigs were kept', so the dale must have been farmed from its earliest days. In the Middle Ages it was owned by the monks of Jervaulx Abbey at the far end of Wensleydale; Grisedale is only about a mile (1.6km) from the River Ure as it begins its decent though Wensleydale. Grisedale seems to have been populated steadily throughout the later centuries, partly because it was adjacent to one of the main routes to the Lake District from the east – Wordsworth recommends the route to Kendal through Wensleydale passing the foot of Grisedale. It also received a boost when the Settle-to-Carlisle railway arrived in 1876. After Round Ing, the walk passes the derelict barns of Flust, where it fords a stream, then continues near the inhabited farmsteads of Fea Fow and East House. It then crosses the ridge with views towards Ingleborough and Whernside, and descends through South Lunds Pasture to Grisedale Crossing on the Settle-to-Carlisle railway line. Beside a typical railway house is a metal footbridge across the line, put up in 1886 to replace an earlier wooden one. Here the line is just below its highest point, 1,169ft (356m), the Ais Gill summit.

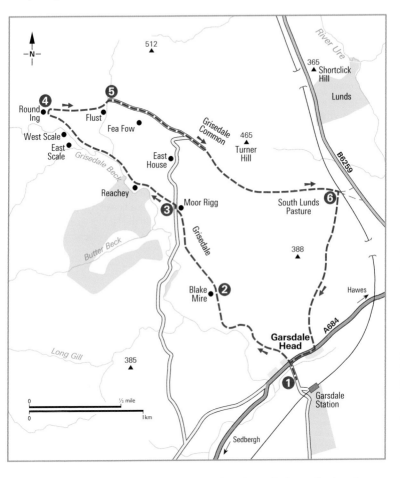

1. Walk down to the main road. Cross at the junction and take a stile signed 'Grisedale and Flust'. Follow a faint path just above the wall on the left, to find another stile in a wall. Follow the sign on a faint path across the moor to another signpost, then descend to another stile right of Blake Mire farmhouse beyond the bend of the wall.

2. Go half right, aiming slightly left of a barn to a gap in a crumbling wall. Continue straight ahead and descend to pass ruined buildings, then turn right, over a stile. Head towards a barn and another stile behind it. Continue to a signpost near a white-painted farmhouse.

3. Cross the lane to another signpost, then down to another stile. From this, bear left near the wall, then descend to follow the beck. Go through a gate and, near the restored house at Reachey, bear right, following waymarkers, to a signposted stile. Follow the beck upstream to a packhorse bridge near deserted East Scale. Do not cross the bridge, but climb by a ruined wall to a gap and fallen signpost. Follow sheep tracks across the moor, aiming for an isolated tree which marks the ruins of Round Ing.

4. At Round Ing double back right, over rising ground to a waymarked post by the corner of a wall. Continue towards the right end of a plantation on the hillside. Go through two gates left of the barn at Flust to join a good track.

5. Follow the track to the junction with a rough metalled lane. Continue ahead on a greener track. This fades, but keep straight ahead over level moorland to a prominent stile on the left and descend the rush-covered, pathless slope beyond. When the slope steepens, aim for the grey footbridge over the railway.

6. Go over a stile beside the railway, pass the footbridge and then cross a stile in a corner close to the line. Walk half right, away from the railway. The path is faint but clear enough. Pass through a tumbled wall and bear lightly left up the steeper slope, then follow the path, bearing slightly right, over the crest to a prominent ladder stile. A clearer path beyond this leads across the slope and soon descends to meet the main road (A684) opposite a line of cottages. It's probably best to cross right away as the verge on the far side is safer. Turn right and walk back to the road junction and the parking place.

Where to eat and drink

The nearest place is the admirable Moorcock Inn a mile (1.6km) east of Garsdale Station on the A684, at its junction with the B6259. It serves lunches, snacks, sandwiches and hot meals at lunchtime.

What to see

Red squirrels have been reported in Garsdale, and refuge sites are being established in conifer woodland to help protect and encourage them. You will be very lucky to spot one, but you may see the tell-tale signs of their presence in the nibbled and discarded pine cones in the woods. There have been red squirrels in Britain since prehistoric times – unlike their larger grey relatives, which came from America in the 1870s. Though the two types sometimes fight, the grey squirrel is more of an opportunist than an invader. Its spread seems to have coincided with a disease that drastically reduced the number of reds in Britain, letting the greys take over the reds' traditional areas.

While you're there

Visit Garsdale Station, the local station for Hawes 6 miles (9.7km) to the east. The station has the only fully operating signal box on the Settle-to-Carlisle line, while just to the south the highest water troughs in the world were once located and trains at speed gathered water from them. The Hawes line closed in 1959 and now forms part of the Dales Countryside Museum.

SEDBERGH AND THE QUAKERS

DISTANCE/TIME	4.5 miles (7.2km) / 1hr 45min
ASCENT/GRADIENT	534ft (163m) / ▲
PATHS	Mostly on field and riverside paths, 7 stiles
LANDSCAPE	Playing fields give way to rich farmland, dominated by fells
SUGGESTED MAP	OS Explorer OL19 Howgill Fells & Upper Eden Valley
START/FINISH	Grid reference: SD659921
DOG FRIENDLINESS	Keep dogs on leads when animals are in fields
PARKING	Pay-and-display car park on Joss Lane, off Sedergh's Main Street (which is one way from the west)
PUBLIC TOILETS	By car park

The solid, stone-built town of Sedbergh, one of the largest settlements in the Yorkshire Dales National Park, was once in the West Riding of Yorkshire, but has been part of Cumbria since 1974. Two things – the Howgill Fells, especially the southernmost peaks of Winder and Crook, and Sedbergh School, which wraps around much of the town's south side – dominate this friendly town. Among its most notable former students are the geologist Adam Sedgwick and the international rugby players Will Carling and Abbie Ward. Brilliant mathematician John Dawson taught Sedgwick and a group of other gifted scholars at the school in the late 18th century, and is commemorated with a bust by the sculptor Flaxman, high on the south nave wall in Sedbergh parish church.

The Quaker link

The Sedbergh area is noted for its Quaker associations. In 1652 the founder of the Society of Friends, George Fox, preached from a bench beneath a yew tree in the churchyard to a great crowd of people attending the Hiring Fair. On Firbank Fell nearby, Fox again preached to a large crowd, this time from a large stone, still known as Fox's Pulpit. This meeting is said to mark the inception of the Society of Friends. Fox wrote: 'This was the place that I had seen a people coming forth in white raiment; and a mighty meeting there was and it is to this day near Sedbergh which I gathered in the name of Jesus.'

Meeting at Brigflatts

The best reminder of the early days of the Quakers in the area is to be found in the tiny hamlet of Brigflatts. Fox stayed here with Richard Robinson in a farmhouse in 1652, and in 1674 the Friends of the district decided to build a Meeting House. It still survives, and is the oldest in the North and the third oldest in England. From the outside, it looks like a typical whitewashed cottage of the period, though, unlike most cottages, it had a stone roof from the start.

Each winter the cracks in the slate were stuffed with moss to stop the rain getting in. George Fox was there in 1677, noting 'a great concourse & there were about 500/600 persons present. A very good meeting it was.' Around the beginning of the 18th century a schoolroom was built over the stable and the gallery was put up to accommodate the large gatherings. At the foot of the gallery stairs look out for the dog pen that was provided for the sheepdogs accompanying their masters to the meetings.

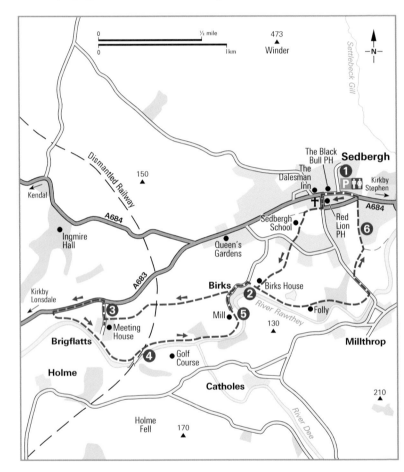

1. From the car park, turn right along Main Street. At the junction with the main road turn left. Just after the churchyard, turn right, signed 'Cattle Market or Busk Lane'. At the next signpost, go left behind the pavilion, then straight ahead through two kissing gates to a road. Cross and go down a track beside playing fields. Go through a kissing gate near a barn and follow a green path to pass Birks House.

2. Go through a kissing gate to a lane and turn left. Pass several houses then go right, through a metal kissing gate, and bear half left to a waymarker, roughly following the Brigflatts sign. Follow the wall and then cross a field to a

small bridge under the old railway. Drop down and bear slightly left on a path across fields to a gate onto a quiet lane opposite the Quaker Burial Ground.

3. Turn left to visit the Meeting House, then return to the gate, continuing on up the lane to the main road. Turn left. Just before the bend sign, go through a signed metal kissing gate in the hedge on the left. Follow the narrow path to meet the River Rawthey and walk upstream to a large railway bridge.

4. Go through the gate and slant up the embankment. Cross and descend back to the river. Continue along the riverside, passing the confluence of the Rawthey and the Dee, and reach a tarmac lane by an old mill.

5. Follow the lane back into Birks. Go right, though the kissing gate signed 'Rawthey Way' (you went through this the other way earlier in the walk). By the hedge around Birks House, bear right and down towards the river. Walk alongside another playing field to a stile. Climb slightly left to go past a folly. Follow the left side of a wood, then enter at a kissing gate. At a footpath sign, bear right down a sunken path. Leave the wood and follow a clear path across a field to emerge onto a road by a bridge. Turn left. By the 'Sedbergh' sign, go right, though a stile. Cross the field to another stile, then bear left alongside a wall to another kissing gate.

6. Cross a drive, go downhill and straight on along a lane to the main road. Cross the road then turn left at the 'No Entry' sign, along Sedbergh's Main Street to the car park.

Where to eat and drink

The Black Bull, The Dalesman Inn and the Red Lion all offer pub meals at lunchtime and evenings on most days of the week. The Three Hares Café on Main Street offers take away hot drinks and food.

What to see

The Howgill Fells, very different from the rest of the Yorkshire Dales, are huge, rounded humps of hills that seem to crowd in on each other like elephants at a watering hole. They are formed from pinkish sandstone and slates, 100 million years older than the limestone that underlies much of the rest of the National Park. The hills have few of the stone walls you will see elsewhere in the Dales – they are mostly common grazing land for the local farms and escaped the passion for enclosure of earlier centuries. One of the spectacular sights of the Dales, the great ribbon of waterfalls known as Cautley Spout is worth the drive from Sedbergh in the direction of Kirkby Stephen – park by the Cross Keys, a temperance inn (it does not sell alcohol). View the falls from there or walk part of the way towards them on a good path.

While you're there

Spend a few quiet minutes in Queen's Gardens in Sedbergh. Described as 'a forgotten Victorian Park', the gardens are west of the town centre, just off the Kendal road. Presented to Sedbergh in 1906 by the splendidly named Mrs Upton-Cottrell-Dormer of Ingmire Hall in memory of Queen Victoria, there are shady trees and specially created glades for wildlife.

DISCOVERING DENT AND DENTDALE

DISTANCE/TIME	5.5 miles (8.8km) / 2hrs 30min
ASCENT/GRADIENT	918ft (280m) / ▲
PATHS	Tracks, field and riverside paths, some roads, 3 stiles
LANDSCAPE	Moorland and farmland, with wide views of Dentdale
SUGGESTED MAP	OS Explorer OL2 Yorkshire Dales – Southern & Western Areas
START/FINISH	Grid reference: SD704871
DOG FRIENDLINESS	On leads in farmland and for riverside sections
PARKING	Pay-and-display car park at west end of Dent
PUBLIC TOILETS	At car park

Dentdale is sometimes called 'the hidden valley'. Unlike most of the Yorkshire Dales it looks west towards the Lake District, and at its western end the limestone landscape gives way suddenly to the rounded Howgill Fells. It seems to have a milder climate and it is more thickly wooded, too. Its 'capital', Dent, is one of the most individual villages of the Dales. Its dog-legged main street is lined with stone cottages that front directly onto the cobbles, or cluster around the church. It is a fascinating spot to explore, with the added benefit of good pubs and tea shops. It is also a busy place in the summer, with tourists and walkers attracted by the special feel of what comedian and walker Mike Harding has called 'the bonniest of all Dales villages'.

Man of the rocks and the terrible knitters

Pride of place on the main street is a drinking fountain made from a huge boulder of Shap granite and simply inscribed 'Adam Sedgwick 1785–1873'. It is a bold and simple memorial to Dent's most famous son. Sedgwick was born in the Old Parsonage by the village green; he was the son of the parson, and the surgeon who delivered him was another Dentdale genius, mathematician John Dawson. Sedgwick went to Sedbergh School and on to Cambridge, where his study of geology, inspired by the rocks of Dentdale, made him among the foremost authorities on the subject. He became Professor of Geology at Cambridge – the university's fascinating geology museum is named after him. He returned regularly to Dent. 'Whenever I have revisited the hills and dales of my native country,' he wrote in 1866, when he was 81, 'I have felt a new swell of emotion, and said to myself, here is the land of my birth; this was the home of my boyhood, and is still the home of my heart.'

Dent was also known for knitting. 'The Terrible Knitters of Dent', the poet Southey called them – intending a compliment on their speed and industry. Men, women and children all knitted – often while engaged in other work. Adam Sedgwick remembered that 'with a speed that cheated the eye they went on with their respective tasks. Beautiful gloves were thrown off complete; and worsted stockings made good progress. There was no dreary noise of machinery; but there was the merry heart-cheering sound of the human tongue.' Dent's woollen socks kept the feet of the British Army warm while they fought Napoleon.

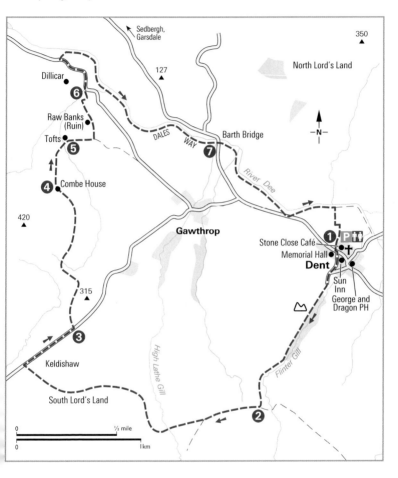

1. Leaving the car park, go up the lane almost opposite, left of the Memorial Hall. Pass the green and keep straight on at the 'Flinter Gill' signpost. The lane becomes a stony track climbing through trees alongside Flinter Gill. Slowly the gradient eases and the trees peter out. Finally you reach a gate beside a seat high on the fellside. Go through the gate to a T-junction of tracks.

2. Turn right, signed 'Keldishaw'. Follow the walled track, for 1.5 miles (2.4km), keeping straight ahead at the only junction. Reaching a tarmac road, turn right for 0.25 miles (400m) to the crest of a rise and a signpost on the left.

3. Go through the gate and follow the grassy track past small shakeholes to a ladder stile. Continue along a dilapidated wall to reach a track. This bears right

below a slope scattered with trees, then contours round with great views of the valley, eventually descending through the yard of a restored farmhouse.

4. Follow the access track winding down the hill, crossing a couple of tumble-down walls before marker posts on the left lead you away from the track. Meet a stream, go left along the bank for a few paces, then cross a simple bridge of two stones. Climb the bank beyond and go straight ahead through a farmyard.

5. Continue down the farm track until it almost levels out alongside a line of trees. Turn sharp left by a large oak, through a waymarked gate. Walk diagonally down the field towards a ruined farmhouse smothered in elder trees. Pass to its right and continue down, soon joining a clearer track. Follow this downhill to reach a drive and go right a few paces to a lane.

6. Turn left along the lane. Follow it round to the right, then back to the left as it levels out in the valley bottom. Watch for a ladder stile by a barn on the left. Don't use this, but look for a signpost on the right, about 50 paces further on, with a plank bridge and stile just below it. From the stile cross the field to the river bank. Go right, following the river (and the Dales Way) upstream for about 0.75 miles (1.2km) to reach stone steps leading to a squeeze stile onto a stone bridge.

7. Go straight across the road and down more steps to continue along the riverside path, until it meets the road. Turn left; the path soon leaves the road again. Follow the riverbank through two more fields, then turn right onto an obvious path. Go through two more fields; at the top of the second turn left, then go right on a track back into the car park.

Where to eat and drink

Dent's two pubs – the much-photographed Sun Inn and the George and Dragon – both serve fine ales and the George and Dragon also serves food, but booking is advisable. The highly recommended Stone Close Café, near the car park, doubles as a National Park information point.

What to see

By the porch of Dent church is the gravestone of George Hodgson, said to have been the Dent Vampire. Born in 1621, George lived to the then-astonishing age of 94. Rumour, even during his lifetime, suggested that his longevity was the result of a pact with the Devil, and that his prominent canine teeth were used for sucking youthful blood from hapless victims. Hedging their bets, the Dent villagers gave him a churchyard burial – but in a remote corner. But when some claimed to have seen his spectre abroad, and blamed some unexplained deaths in the dale on it, they dug him up and reburied him, with a stake through his heart, by the porch.

While you're there

The Sedgwick Geological Trail beside the A684 in Garsdale, tells you more about Adam Sedgwick and his geological discoveries. It takes you into the valley of the Clough River and explains how the line of the Dent Fault, first identified by Sedgwick, can be traced by the marked differences of the landscape.

COWGILL AND THE RIVER DEE

DISTANCE/TIME	3.5 miles (5.7km) / 1hr 30min
ASCENT/GRADIENT	131ft (40m) / ▲
PATHS	Tracks, field and riverside paths, some roads, 17 stiles
LANDSCAPE	Lush valley bottom, views of the fells and farmland
SUGGESTED MAP	OS Explorer OL2 Yorkshire Dales – Southern & Western Areas
START/FINISH	Grid reference: SD742864
DOG FRIENDLINESS	Keep under close control; lots of stiles
PARKING	Parking place at Ibbeth Peril
PUBLIC TOILETS	None on route

Cowgill, near the narrow head of Dentdale, is a cluster of houses alongside the River Dee. Now mostly an agricultural, holiday and residential settlement, in the past it housed both miners and mill workers – near Ewegales Bridge was Dee Mill, where worsteds were spun at the beginning of the 19th century. The fast-flowing Dee, which may be named after a Celtic river goddess, and in turn gives its name to Dentdale, provided the power; it tumbles and slides across limestone terraces and through gorges on its way to join the River Rawthey near Sedbergh. Though innocent in good weather, the river can be fierce after rain – in 1870 Ewegales Bridge and Lea Yeat Bridge, both on the walk, were swept away.

Perilous undertaking
The start of the walk crosses a footbridge over the river as it rushes through a gorge where there is a waterfall called Ibbeth Peril. The waterfall has a cave (reputedly the home of a witch called Ibby) behind it – just one of a series of caves and passages that riddle the limestone in this part of the dale. Much favoured by speleologists, access to the main system (for the experienced only) is through a narrow entrance in the riverbank, which leads to a passage eventually opening into a large cavern. Other caverns and underground waterfalls lie beyond, though the whole system has yet to be explored in full.

The Queen intervenes
St John's Church at Cowgill, seen across the river near Ewegales Bridge, owes much to geologist Adam Sedgwick. His sister started a Sunday school in Cowgill and soon there was a pressing need for a church. Sedgwick himself laid the foundation stone in 1837, when a crowd of 700 gathered in celebration. However, the early days of the chapel were not straightforward; diocesan officials first failed to register it as a place of worship, then called it by the wrong name. It took the personal intervention of Queen Victoria – Sedgwick had been a close acquaintance of Prince Albert – to sort out the mess.

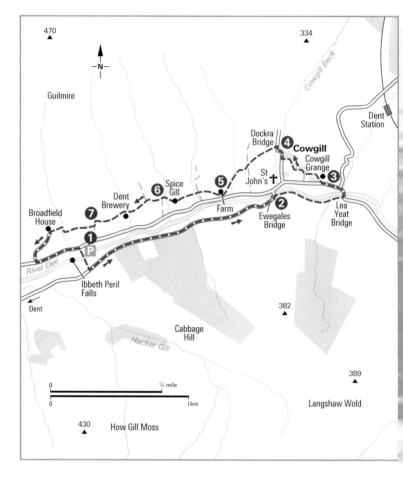

1. Opposite the car park entrance, a short footpath leads to a footbridge. Cross, then head across the field to a gate and turn left along the road. Follow the road for 1 mile (1.6km) until you get to a stone bridge over the River Dee.

2. Don't cross the bridge, but go over a stile signed 'Lea Yeat' and continue along the riverside path until a wooden stile leads onto Lea Yeat Bridge. Cross the bridge, then turn left at the signpost towards Dent and Sedbergh.

3. Just beyond the postbox on the left, follow a sign on the right to Dockra Bridge. Go a short way up the drive for Cowgill Grange, then bear left behind another house to a stile. Continue to walk below another house, then bear right to a gate. Continue through more gates to skirt left of another house and out to a track. Go right and soon reach Dockra Bridge.

4. Cross the bridge, bend right, then go over a stile on your left. Go half left to a stile in a crossing wall. Continue with a wall on your left and cross a track to a waymarked gate. Go right of a barn, through a gateway below a power line and then cross a small stream. Bear left across a field to a signpost and stile by a farm.

5. Go half right to another stile. Continue along a wall to another stile and a footbridge, then head towards farm buildings. Follow the track through the farmyard, then turn right immediately after the farmhouse, before a stone barn. Go left behind the barn to a bridge with steps and a gated stile beyond.

6. Cross the field to another stile in the corner. Just beyond, turn right along a track. As it bends right, go straight ahead to pass below a house and down to a gate. Go round behind another house to a wooden stile. Go ahead across the field to a stone stile, then go left of the barn onto a track over a stream.

7. Curve round left of the next barn and follow the wall. At the next farm buildings, go through a metal gate by a barn, then follow the walled, often wet, track bending right. At the next gate bear left, go through a stile, go to the right of the farm building and onto a track. Turn right, and then bear left through a waymarked gate, pass the farmhouse and follow the track to the road. Turn left to return to the car park; you can join a parallel path through the trees near the end.

Where to eat and drink
There is nowhere on the route, but nearby Dent has two pubs and a selection of tea rooms, or go east towards Dent Head viaduct for The Sportsman's Inn, which serves bar meals. (Closed Mondays and only serves food in the evenings).

What to see
While on the first, eastward, part of the walk, look up to the facing hillside to see the white-painted Victorian buildings of Dent Station – the highest mainline railway station in England. It is 1,132ft (345m) above sea level and is one of the stops on the spectacular Settle-to-Carlisle line. While it can be an inhospitable place when the winds blow and the winter storms set in, it proved a way into the wider world for the people of Dentdale – even though to reach it from Dent meant a 4-mile (6.4km) walk and a stiff climb. In the later part of his life it was the route regularly taken by Adam Sedgwick on his way to and from York to reach London or Cambridge. It is still used by local people – you may see them walking along the valley roads carrying their supermarket shopping from Settle or Carlisle. And you will certainly hear the whistle of the trains as they pass over Dent Head and Arten Gill viaducts as they approach Dent Station.

While you're there
Visit Dent Brewery, which you pass on the walk between points 6 and 7. It is not open to casual visitors – so don't just drop in – but visits are available every Saturday, starting from The George and Dragon in Dent, with transport to the brewery. You can sample some of the Brewery's prize-winning beers, many with sheep-related names such as Sheep and Shearful, Baarister and Ewe are the Weakest Link.

KIRKBY LONSDALE AND THE RIVER LUNE

DISTANCE/TIME	4.75 miles (7.7km) / 2hrs 30min
ASCENT/GRADIENT	197ft (60m) / ▲
PATHS	A little overgrown and indistinct in patches, quiet lanes and tracks, 12 stiles
LANDSCAPE	Rolling hills, farmland, riverbank, good distance views
SUGGESTED MAP	OS Explorer OL2 Yorkshire Dales – Southern & Western Areas
START/FINISH	Grid reference: SD615782
DOG FRIENDLINESS	On leads through farmland
PARKING	Either side of Devil's Bridge, Kirkby Lonsdale
PUBLIC TOILETS	At the start on the town side of Devil's Bridge

It's something of a revelation to escape the weekend motorcycle congregation on Devil's Bridge and take this circular walk over rolling hills, through farmland and woods, to the village of Whittington, then to return along the banks of the lovely Lune. You pass close to Sellet Mill – its huge waterwheel, incorporated within the building, was reputedly once the second largest in the country. Corn was ground at the mill until its closure in the 1940s.

Sellet is a word you'll come across often on this walk and is apparently an old local word for drumlin (a small rounded hill formed by glacial deposits). Your next Sellet is Sellet Bank, which appears to be a large drumlin. The walk takes you around its base and eventually to Sellet Hall. Built as a farm in 1570 by the Baines family, the hall was possibly used at one time as a hospital, as it is situated at the end of Hosticle Lane – hosticle is a dialect word for hospital. You return to Kirkby Lonsdale along the banks of the River Lune, following part of the Lune Valley Ramble.

The river and Devil's Bridge

A simple spring in a field at Newbiggin-on-Lune is the source of the beautiful River Lune, which eventually flows into Morecambe Bay and the Irish Sea to the north of Cockersand Abbey. The river has inspired many artists, most famously J M W Turner, who visited Kirkby Lonsdale in 1818 and subsequently included the river in two paintings.

Devil's Bridge is so called because it was supposedly provided by the Devil to enable a poor widow to reach her cow on the other side of the river in return for him acquiring the soul of the first being to cross the bridge. The widow's only other possession was a small dog. According to a 1920s poem, she threw a bun across the bridge and the poor hound scampered after it, thwarting the Devil and saving her own soul. This graceful, three-arched structure probably dates from the 14th century and no longer has to support the busy A65, which has had its own river crossing downstream since the 1930s.

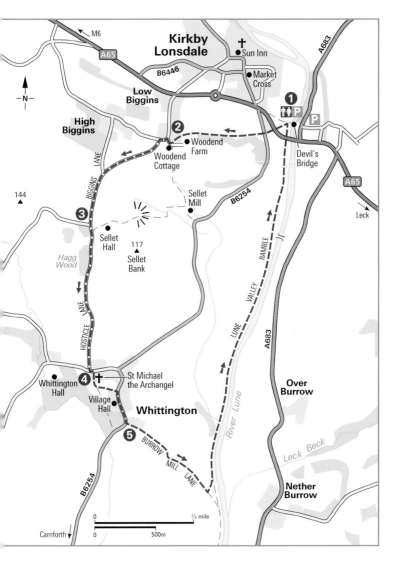

1. From the west bank of the river, a few paces downstream from Devil's Bridge, go diagonally up across a park with picnic tables to a kissing gate near paired conifers. Cross the A65, go through a narrow meadow and between houses and cross the B6254. As you enter another meadow, go uphill, keeping the walled wooded area on your left. Yellow markers help you find the route. Keep on over the brow of the hill and straight ahead through two kissing gates to a metal gate near houses. Bear left to a signpost.

2. Cross a farm track to the white-painted Woodend Cottage. Turn right here and follow the track to the road. At the road turn left and follow it down. At a junction on the right, the road becomes Biggins Lane.

3. Just before Sellet Hall comes into view on the left, a road branches out to the right. Stay straight ahead towards Whittington village along the road that is now called Hosticle Lane. The lane is sunken in places and carries very little traffic. The descent steepens as you approach the outskirts of Whittington.

4. Go left at the T-junction for a few paces, then cross the road and turn right over a pebbled mosaic at the entrance to the Church of St Michael the Archangel. Keep the square bell tower on your left before descending stone steps to go through a narrow stile and the modern graveyard. Follow the hedge to a gate in the left corner and keep straight on to reach a stone stile into a walled path that leads onto Main Street. Turn right and walk through the village past the village hall.

5. At a sharp right bend on the edge of the village, turn left along a gritty track, passing a farm and tennis courts. Follow the lane as it winds between fields, eventually crossing a cattle grid and running out at an anglers' hut beside the Lune. Follow the riverbank upstream on the route of the Lune Valley Ramble. There's a short overgrown section but it soon becomes an easy walk through fields, always close to the river. The route is obvious back to the A65 bridge at Kirkby Lonsdale. Go through a gate and up steps to the left of the parapet. Cross the road and drop down the other side to cross the park at the start of the walk.

Where to eat and drink

There are usually a couple of vans at Devil's Bridge, one selling ices and the other selling drinks and snacks. The Sun Inn is a splendid 5-star boutique inn in Kirkby Lonsdale and serves a selection of hot and cold food. There are numerous other food outlets in the town from cafés and pubs to fish and chips for take away.

What to see

Leck Fell at 2,058ft (627m) is the highest point in present-day Lancashire (although Coniston Old Man is the highest point in the 'old' Lancashire). The fell is worth visiting for its limestone scenery and archaeological sites, while below ground is a popular network of caving systems.

While you're there

Visit Kirkby Lonsdale, which gained its market charter in the 13th century and still holds a weekly market, around the unusual 20th-century market cross, every Thursday. There are some fine 17th- and 18th-century buildings and some famous views from the churchyard.

RIBBLEHEAD VIADUCT AND BLEA MOOR

14

DISTANCE/TIME	5 miles (8km) / 2hrs
ASCENT/GRADIENT	328ft (100m) / ▲
PATHS	Moorland and farm paths and tracks, 1 stile
LANDSCAPE	Bleak moorland and farmland, dominated by the Ribblehead Viaduct
SUGGESTED MAP	OS Explorer OL2 Yorkshire Dales – Southern & Western Areas
START/FINISH	Grid reference: SD766793
DOG FRIENDLINESS	Dogs can be off leads by viaduct, but should be on leads on farmland
PARKING	Parking area at junction of B6255 and B6479 near Ribblehead Viaduct
PUBLIC TOILETS	None on route

'Nowhere in the kingdom has nature placed such gigantic obstacles in the way of the railway engineer,' observed a newspaper when the Settle-to-Carlisle railway line was complete. The railway was planned and built by the Midland Railway so it could reach Scotland without trespassing on its rivals' east and west coast routes. Opened in 1876, it cost the then-enormous sum of £3.5 million. Its construction included building 20 big viaducts and 14 tunnels. At the height of the works 6,000 men were employed, living in shanty towns beside the line and giving the area a flavour of the Wild West. The line survived for almost 100 years, until passenger services were withdrawn in 1970 among claims that Ribblehead was unsafe. A public outcry led to a campaign to keep the line open. Ribblehead is now repaired, and the line is one of the most popular – and spectacular – tourist railways in the country.

Ribblehead – 'a mighty work'

It took five years to build Ribblehead's huge viaduct. It is 0.25 miles (400m) long, and up to 100ft (30m) high; the columns stretch another 25ft (7.6m) into the ground. The stone – more than 30,000 cubic yards (22,950 cubic metres) of it – came from Littledale. The columns are rumoured to be set on bales of wool, as the engineers could not find the bedrock. This, romantic as it is in a county whose fortunes are largely based on wool, is untrue; they are set in concrete on top of the rock. There are 24 spans, each 45ft (13.7m) wide. Every sixth column is thicker than its neighbours so that if one column fell it would take only five others with it, and not the whole viaduct.

Blea Moor and ancient farms

The walk takes you near perhaps the most exposed signal box in Britain. Beyond it is Blea Moor tunnel, another of the mighty engineering works of the Settle-to-Carlisle Railway, 2,629yds (2,404m) long and dug by miners, their work lit by candlelight.

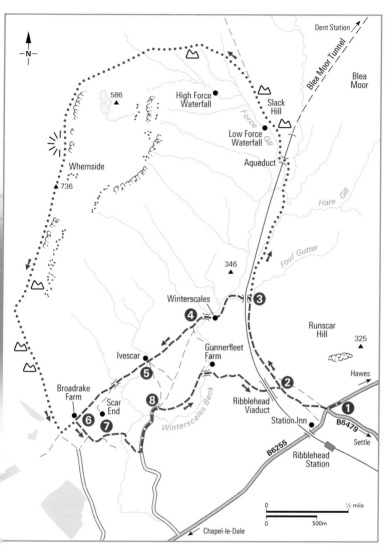

1. From your parking place near the road junction, with the B6479 at your back, follow green paths towards the viaduct. Turn right on a gravel track and follow it until it turns under the viaduct; continue walking straight ahead.

2. Walk parallel with the railway line above you to your left, past a Three Peaks signboard. Go through a gate and continue until you reach a railway signal. Go left under the railway arch, following the public bridleway sign.

3. Follow the track downhill towards the stream, then bear left, roughly parallel to the water, to Winterscales. Go through a gate between the buildings and onto a humpback bridge below a cottage.

4. Follow the lane over a cattle grid then fork right (almost straight ahead). Keep left at the next fork, pass an isolated cowshed and continue to Ivescar

farm. Pass in front of the house and after a few paces bear left through a waymarked gate.

5. Walk along a track through fields and cross a small bridge made of railway sleepers. Immediately after this, bear right to a small gate. Cross a series of fields, keeping a straight course, to reach Broadrake Farm.

6. Turn left down the farm track. Where it bends right, go over the cattle grid and turn sharp left round the fence and onto a track, following the bridleway sign, to a ladder stile.

7. The obvious track winds through fields to reach a streambed (usually dry in summer). Cross this, which can be tricky after prolonged wet weather. The track is a little indistinct after the crossing, but bear right, staying near the stream until it becomes clear again. Meet a road near a cattle grid, turn left and walk down the road and over a bridge.

8. Where the road divides, go right through a gate towards the viaduct. At the next gate, go right again over a footbridge by the farm buildings. Continue along the track and go under the viaduct, then retrace your steps back to the parking area.

Extending the walk You can extend this walk to take in one of the famous Three Peaks, Whernside. From Point 3, follow the signpost towards Dent. Cross over two streams and then the railway by a bridge alongside an aqueduct. Go through a gate, and at a signpost continue ahead for Dentdale (not Dent Head). The path ascends past a waterfall, then climbs steeply to a stile on your left. Turn left over the stile, following the Whernside sign. The path meets a wall on the right and a paved section climbs to the ridge. Continue along the ridge to the summit, then follow the same path steeply downhill to reach two gated stiles, then a pair of ladder stiles flanking a farm gate. Continue down to a farm gate beside a barn, then turn left, signed 'Winterscales'. Follow the path through the field towards the farm. Go through a gate to rejoin the main walk at Point 6.

Where to eat and drink

In the summer an ice cream and burger van is at the parking area by the road junction, and it's usually there at weekends in winter too for hot drinks and snacks. The Station Inn, near the viaduct, offers warmth and home-cooked meals in its bar and dining room.

What to see

On a fine summer's day Ribblehead can seem magical, but it can be one of the bleakest places in the Dales. The average rainfall in the area is 70 inches (177.8cm) and snow frequently blocks the roads. Wind speeds of 50 knots are normal, and gales can reach a greater speed.

While you're there

Take the road or train up to Dent Station. You will pass through the Blea Moor tunnel and then over the Dent Head viaduct, with its 10 spans, and the same maximum height as Ribblehead.

15

HUBBERHOLME AND LANGSTROTHDALE

DISTANCE/TIME	5.25 miles (8.4km) / 2hrs
ASCENT/GRADIENT	480ft (146m) / ▲ ▲
PATHS	Field paths and tracks, steep after Yockenthwaite, 11 stiles
LANDSCAPE	Streamside paths and limestone terrace
SUGGESTED MAP	OS Explorer OL30 Yorkshire Dales - Northern & Central Areas
START/FINISH	Grid reference: SD927782
DOG FRIENDLINESS	Dogs should be on leads, except on section between Yockenthwaite and Cray
PARKING	Beside river in village, opposite church (not church parking)
PUBLIC TOILETS	None on route, but nearby in Buckden

Literary pilgrims visit Hubberholme to see The George Inn, where J B Priestley could often be found enjoying the local ale, and the churchyard, the last resting place for his ashes as he requested. He chose an idyllic spot. Set at the foot of Langstrothdale, Hubberholme is a cluster of old farmhouses and cottages surrounding the church. Norman in origin, St Michael's was once flooded so badly that fish were seen swimming in the nave. One vicar of Hubberholme is said to have carelessly baptised a child Amorous instead of Ambrose, a mistake that, once entered in the parish register, couldn't be altered.

Church wood

Hubberholme church's best treasures are made of wood. The rood loft above the screen is one of only two surviving in Yorkshire (the other is at Flamborough, far away on the east coast). Once holding figures of Christ on the Cross, St Mary and St John, it dates from 1558, when such examples of Popery were fast going out of fashion. It still retains some of its colouring of red, gold and black. Master-carver Robert Thompson provided almost all the rest of the furniture in 1934 – look for his mouse trademark.

Ancient Yockenthwaite and remote Cray

Yockenthwaite's name, said to have been derived from an ancient Irish name, Eogan, conjures up images of the ancient past. Norse settlers were here more than 1,000 years ago and even earlier settlers have left their mark – a Bronze Age stone circle a little further up the valley. The hamlet now consists of a few farm buildings beside the bridge over the Wharfe at the end of Langstrothdale Chase, a Norman hunting ground which used to have its own forest laws and punishments. You walk along a typical Dales limestone terrace to reach Cray, on the road over from Bishopdale joining Wharfedale to Wensleydale. Here is another huddle of farmhouses, around The White Lion Inn. You then follow the Cray Gill downstream past a series of small cascades. For a more spectacular waterfall, head a little way up the road from the inn to Cray High Bridge.

Burning the candle

Back in Hubberholme, The George Inn was once the vicarage. Each New Year's Day, an ancient auction there begins with the lighting of a candle, before the auctioneer asks for bids for the year's tenancy of the 'Poor Pasture', a 16-acre (6.5ha) field behind the inn. All bids have to be completed before the candle burns out. A merry time is had by all and the proceeds go to help the older people of the village.

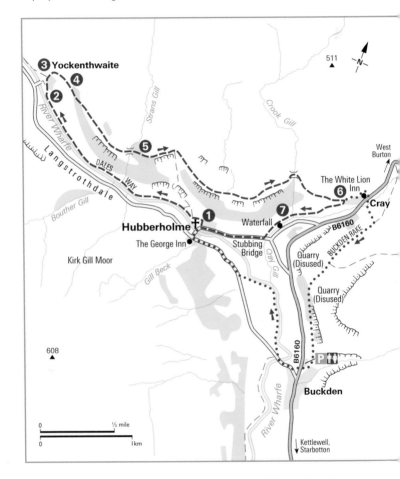

1. Enter the farmyard beside the church and turn left immediately through a gate signed 'Dales Way'. Take the lower path, signed 'Yockenthwaite', alongside the churchyard. Walk beside the river for 1.25 miles (2km); the clear Dales Way path is never far from the river. Approaching Yockenthwaite, go up steps to a little gate and left to a gate and signpost.

2. Follow the track towards a bridge but, before reaching it, go sharp right up a farm track, which swings back left to a sign to Cray and Hubberholme.

3. Go up to another signpost, then follow the obvious track slanting right and up. Part-way up the hill, go right at a footpath sign through a gate.

4. Follow the near-level path to a signpost, then bear left and up a rough section to another signpost. Turn right and follow the obvious path, descending along a beautiful natural terrace until the path goes left and up to enter a wood by a footbridge over a miniature gorge.

5. Walk through the wood then continue, level again, to reach a small side valley above a house. A signpost above the house points towards Cray. Go up slightly, over rocks, then along another green terrace path for about a mile (1.6km) to a footbridge. Cross this, then ascend slightly to a barn; bear right to a gate then follow a marked path across meadow land. Go past a house to a junction of tracks on the edge of Cray.

6. Go sharp right, down to a footpath sign to Stubbing Bridge. Descend between stone walls and through a gate and onto the grassy hillside. Pass another footpath sign and continue downhill to meet the stream.

7. Follow the streamside path past waterfalls and pools, crossing a stone bridge over a side-stream. Cross a stile and continue past a barn to reach the road. Turn right to return to the parking area in Hubberholme.

Extending the walk You can see more of the beautiful Upper Wharfedale scenery by extending the walk from Cray to the peaceful village of Buckden. From Point 6 on the main walk, follow a metalled road to The White Lion Inn, then cross the valley and climb to Buckden Rake. Descend this to Buckden before returning to the parking area at Hubberholme via the Dales Way.

Where to eat and drink

The George Inn in Hubberholme has an enviable reputation for its food and real ale, as well as its convivial atmosphere. The same is true of The White Lion Inn at Cray – slightly off the route.

What to see

A number of barns in the area have been converted into holiday accommodation bunk barns. An initiative set up by the Yorkshire Dales National Park Authority and the Countryside Commission in 1979, the aim is to solve two problems – how to preserve the now-redundant barns that are so vital a part of the Dales landscape, and a lack of simple accommodation for walkers. Farmers add basic amenities to the barns for cooking, washing and sleeping and let them out to families or groups at a realistic nightly rate.

While you're there

Nearby Buckden Pike has fine views and a memorial to five Polish airmen whose plane crashed there in November 1942. One man survived, following a fox's footprints through the snow down to safety at a farm. The cross he erected in thanksgiving has a fox's head set in the base. Buckden Pike is best climbed using the track called Walden Road from Starbotton.

HORSEHOUSE AND COVERDALE

DISTANCE/TIME	6.5 miles (10.4km) / 2hrs 30min
ASCENT/GRADIENT	418ft (128m) / ▲
PATHS	Field, moorland and riverside paths and tracks, 31 stiles
LANDSCAPE	Farmed valley and moorland, with River Cover
SUGGESTED MAP	OS Explorer OL30 Yorkshire Dales - Northern & Central Areas
START/FINISH	Grid reference: SE047813
DOG FRIENDLINESS	Sheep in fields, so keep dogs on leads
PARKING	Roadside parking below former school in Horsehouse
PUBLIC TOILETS	None on route

It seems hard to believe that the quiet village of Horsehouse once bustled with stagecoaches and packhorse trains on one of the main coaching routes from London to the North. The two village inns served the travellers on their way to and from Richmond, one of the region's principal coaching centres.

Beyond Horsehouse, to the southwest, Coverdale grows steeper and wilder before the vertiginous descent down Park Rash into Kettlewell in Wharfedale. Travellers and trains of up to 40 packhorses used the route, bringing goods to the valley and taking lead and other minerals from the mines on the moors above. Bells jingling on the harness of the leading horse signalled their presence.

Headless pedlars and a future king

Pedlars, too, followed the routes, and some met a gruesome end; three headless corpses were found by a road into Nidderdale. The evidence suggested that they were Scottish pedlars, killed for their money and goods. Their heads were not found – nor were their murderers, though local suspicion pointed strongly at a Horsehouse innkeeper and her daughter.

West Scrafton, a tiny village set beside Great Gill as it tumbles towards the River Cover below, is dominated by Great Roova Crags (1,549ft/472m). Before the dissolution of the monasteries in the 1530s, the village was owned by the monks of Jervaulx Abbey. Much of the land was subsequently in the hands of the Earl of Lennox – and West Scrafton Manor House is said to have been the birthplace of his son Lord Darnley, murdered second husband of Mary, Queen of Scots and father of King James I and VI.

Carlton-in-Coverdale (or Carlton), the next village, has the motte of a small castle visible south of the main street. Flatts Farm at the west end of the village has an inscription to Henry Constantine, 'The Coverdale Poet'.

Miles Coverdale, the first man to translate the whole Bible into English, was born in the valley – no one knows where – in 1488. The first edition was published in 1535, and a revised version, known as the Great Bible, in 1538.

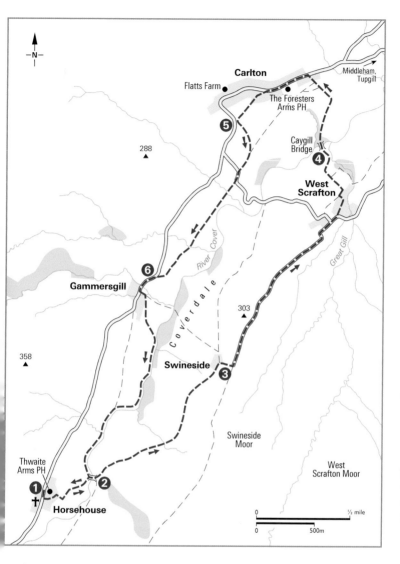

1. Walk past the Thwaite Arms, then curve behind it on a track between houses. Turn right down a signed track through a garden. Go through two gates, bend left to a third gate, then bear half right to a gate. Then continue to a footbridge.

2. Cross the bridge and bear left, uphill. Go over a stile signed 'Swineside', cross a small field to another stile, then bear half right to go through a small plantation. Keep on in the same direction across open land, crossing a small stream, to a stile, then on to another stile and footpath sign. Bear left across a field to a gap in the left-hand boundary, then contour along a path, which becomes clearer as you go, and cross a stile just above the first building of Swineside Farm.

3. Follow the track past the farmhouse then right, uphill. At the top, cross a cattle grid and follow the metalled lane for 1.5 miles (2.4km) into West Scrafton. In the village take a track to the left marked as a dead end. Turn left, signed 'Carlton', and follow the walled path round to the right. At its end turn left (footpath sign) down a field. Go through a kissing gate and down to a fingerpost. Turn right down a clear track signed to Caygill Bridge. Follow the field edge to two footbridges.

4. After the bridges, go through a gate and ascend a steep path into a field. Turn left at a signpost, then turn right alongside a wall and on to a gate. Follow a clear path between walls to the road in Carlton. Turn left, passing The Foresters Arms. Where it widens, bear left, then turn left at a footpath sign and cross a stile. Continue straight ahead over stiles to a road.

5. Turn left and go immediately through a gate. Descend to a stile, bear right to another stile and follow a wall to a stile onto a road. Turn left. At a left bend, go right, over a stile signed 'Gammersgill'. Go over two more stiles and cross a footbridge. Continue ahead to a waymarked gate. Cross the fields, going over a stile and a wooden footbridge, and enter a walled lane. At a sharp right bend, go ahead through a stile, then bear right to a stile onto the road.

6. Turn left into Gammersgill, cross the bridge, then turn left though a gate signed 'Swineside'. Bear right to another gate, then cross to a stile beside a gate. Bear half left to the field corner and go over a stile. Now follow the river until you reach the footbridge crossed near the start of the walk. Retrace your steps back to Horsehouse.

Where to eat and drink

The Thwaite Arms in Horsehouse has a friendly atmosphere but is only open in the evening during the week and for a short lunchtime period at the weekends. The Foresters Arms in Carlton is famous for its fine meals and is worth a special journey.

What to see

Like Middleham at the end of the valley, Coverdale is much given over to horses, with riding schools and livery stables throughout the dale. This is not a recent phenomenon – in writer Daniel Defoe's day the whole area was geared to the horse; in the third volume of his *A Tour through the Whole Island of Great Britain*, published in 1726, he wrote that 'all this country is full of jockeys, that is to say, dealers in horses, and breeders of horses.'

While you're there

Visit The Forbidden Corner, a fantasy garden full of follies, tunnels, secret chambers and passages offering intrigue and unexpected discoveries. Built by a former British Ambassador to Ecuador at Tupgill, 3 miles (4.8km) east of Carlton, The Forbidden Corner is open by timed ticket in advance only. Book via theforbiddencorner.co.uk, phone 01969 640638 or at the tourist information centre in Leyburn.

RIPON ROWEL WALK NEAR MASHAM

DISTANCE/TIME	4 miles (6.4km) / 2hrs
ASCENT/GRADIENT	566ft (173m) / ▲
PATHS	Tracks and field paths, 7 stiles
LANDSCAPE	Valley and farmland, with some surprising constructions
SUGGESTED MAP	OS Explorer 298 Nidderdale
START/FINISH	Grid reference: SE177787
DOG FRIENDLINESS	Keep dogs on leads or under close control
PARKING	Car park by Druid's Temple
PUBLIC TOILETS	None on route

Start or finish the walk with a druidical flourish by visiting the Druid's Temple – one of the most extraordinary of Yorkshire's rich crop of follies. It was created on the orders of William Danby, eccentric master of nearby Swinton Castle, in 1809. One of his purposes was philanthropy – there was widespread unemployment in Nidderdale, and he saw his version of Stonehenge as a job creation scheme. What his workers thought when they were paid to build something so strange is not recorded.

The hermit and the luminous moss

Danby's Druid's Temple bears only superficial resemblance to Stonehenge. It is oval, not round, and sits in a hollow, solidly lined with great upright stones. Opposite the entrance is a cave, said to contain a rare luminous moss. Outside the temple, like tugs around an ocean liner, are pretend cromlechs, huge flat stones on uprights. These betray the early 19th-century origins of the temple – they are spaced with perfect symmetry, in the best classical tradition. Less classical, though very fashionable, was the hermit who is said to have inhabited the cave for four and a half years, without cutting his hair or beard.

The walk passes through what was perhaps a trial run for the splendours of the Druid's Temple, a gateway of massively piled boulders, before descending towards the valley of the Pott Beck – a reminder that the area, for council purposes, goes under the delightful name of Ilton-cum-Pott. You will see the dam wall of Leighton Reservoir ahead (you can see the reservoir itself from just beyond the Druid's Temple). It was under construction at the outbreak of World War I and then the site was taken over by the 1st Leeds Battalion – the Leeds Pals – who were stationed here for nine months, before being transferred first to Ripon, then, via Hampshire and Egypt, to the Somme.

Spurring on

Much of the walk follows the Ripon Rowel Walk, a 50-mile (80km) circular route centred on the city of Ripon, and officially starting from the cathedral. It is, appropriately, named after the rowels – the small spiked wheels that fitted to the back of a horse rider's spurs – that were Ripon's speciality in the

16th and 17th centuries. So renowned were the rowels manufactured here that a royal charter recognised their superiority, and they gave rise to a common folk saying 'As true steel as Ripon rowels'. A spur is in the city's coat of arms (along with a horn) and can be seen on the top of the 300-year-old obelisk in the Market Square. Many local clubs and societies also use this symbol in their emblems and even their titles. The Ripon Rowel Walk is well waymarked by a spiked wheel symbol.

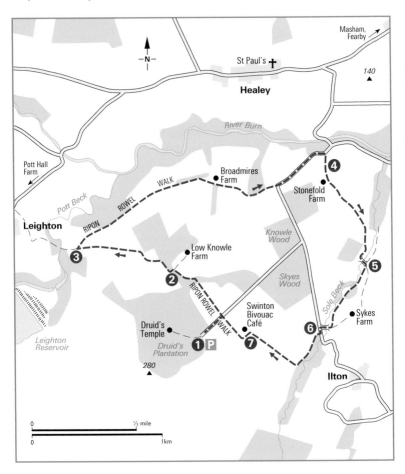

1. Park in the car park by the Druid's Temple (to visit the temple, walk though the wood, then return to the car park) and walk down the road you drove up. Just after a row of metal posts, cross a stile on the left marked with the Ripon Rowel Walk symbol, opposite a track leading to Swinton Bivouac. Walk ahead across the field and go though a gate surrounded by boulders. Bend left, along the edge of the wood and at the farm track, go left to a gate.

2. After the gate turn right, following the track. It bends away from the wood and down to a ladder stile. After the stile, bear half left across the field towards the pine trees to a stile in a crossing wire fence. Continue ahead,

bearing slightly left, to descend by a small wood to two stout wooden posts, one of them waymarked.

3. At the posts turn sharp right, uphill, on the grassy track. Follow the rutted track, mostly level, until it passes to the right of Broadmires farm. The track becomes stony and then leads straight out into a metalled lane. At a road junction continue straight ahead, now descending. On a bend, turn right through a metal gate towards Stonefold farm.

4. Walk past the farmhouse, and turn left through a gate to a small enclosure. Cross a stile and go a few paces to another stile. From this bear right to a gate, then continue ahead to a waymarked post. Bear right across the field through a gateway in a crossing fence and pick up a descending track, which bears right. Below a plantation, leave the track and cross a stile on the left. Follow a narrow path to another stile and a footbridge just beyond.

5. Cross the bridge and go over a waymarked stile, then turn right, along a track. Go through two gates, past a barn, and through another metal gate on to a lane.

6. Turn left, then turn right on the next track. Go over a stile beside a gate, and along the track. After a gateway, turn right alongside a wall, climbing towards the farm on the ridge. Approaching the farm, cross a stile in a wire fence.

7. After the stile, bend to the left, following a wooden fence, in front of the farm building, then through a metal gate on your right-hand side. Follow the farm track and exit onto the metalled lane over a stile by the gate. Turn left back to the car park.

Where to eat and drink

The Swinton Bivouac, which you pass on the walk, has an excellent café. A visit to Masham also offers a good choice of both pubs and cafés. The Bar and Kitchen in the Black Sheep Brewery is recommended. The Black Swan at Fearby also serves good meals with an emphasis on local produce (hours may be limited in winter).

What to see

As you approach Broadmires farm, look across the valley to the village of Healey and its extraordinary church. St Paul's was designed in 1848 by Edward Buckton Lam, who rejected the current ideas of historical precedent and worked entirely for picturesque effect. St Paul's has big ideas, with a central tower and transepts, as well as a spire. Inside it has the most amazing timberwork, like the inside of a mad ship – a wooden, ecclesiastical equivalent of William Danby's Druid's Temple.

While you're there

Island Heritage at Pott Hall Farm by Leighton Reservoir has a wide range of primitive, domesticated sheep from around Britain, including Hebridean, Manx Loghtan and Shetland. According to the season you can see young lambs, watch the shearing or see the fleeces being sorted for spinning (call 01765 689651 to check).

DISCOVERING SOWERBY AND THIRSK

DISTANCE/TIME	5.75 miles (9.25km) / 2hrs 15min
ASCENT/GRADIENT	207ft (63m) / ▲
PATHS	Town paths, field paths and tracks, 4 stiles
LANDSCAPE	Streamside and undulating pastureland around town
SUGGESTED MAP	OS Explorer 302 Northallerton & Thirsk
START/FINISH	Grid reference: SE431813
DOG FRIENDLINESS	Dogs should be on leads
PARKING	Roadside parking on Front Street in Sowerby village
PUBLIC TOILETS	Thirsk town centre

The elegant Georgian village street of Sowerby – now joined on to the town of Thirsk – is lined with a handsome avenue of lime trees. Such a civilised aspect belies the origins of the village's name, for Sowerby means the 'township in the muddy place'. Once you begin the walk, the reason becomes evident, even in dry weather. Sowerby is on the edge of the flood plain of the Cod Beck. Sowerby Flatts, which you will see across the beck at the start of the walk, and cross at the finish, is a popular venue for impromptu games of football and other sports, but is still prone to flooding.

Between old and new

Once you've crossed the road by the end of New Bridge, you are walking between Old Thirsk and New Thirsk – though new in this context still means medieval. Old Thirsk is set to the east of the Cod Beck; like Sowerby, it too has a watery name, for Thirsk comes from an old Swedish word meaning a 'fen'. New Thirsk, to the west, is centred on the fine cobbled market place. The parish church, which you will pass twice, is the best Perpendicular church in North Yorkshire, with a particularly imposing tower.

South Kilvington, at the northern end of the walk, used to be a busy village on the main road north from Thirsk to Yarm. For much of the 19th century it was home to William Kingsley, who was vicar here until his death at the age of 101 in 1916 – having been born as Wellington defeated Napoleon at Waterloo.

Darrowby and Wight

For many visitors, the essential place to visit in Thirsk is Skeldale House in Kirkgate – on the right as you return from the church to the Market Square. This was the surgery of local vet Alf Wight – better known by his pen name, James Herriot. Now an award-winning museum, The World of James Herriot, this was where Wight worked for all his professional life. Thirsk itself is a major character in the books, appearing lightly disguised as Darrowby. The museum has reconstructions of what the surgery and the family rooms were like in the 1940s, and tells the history of veterinary science.

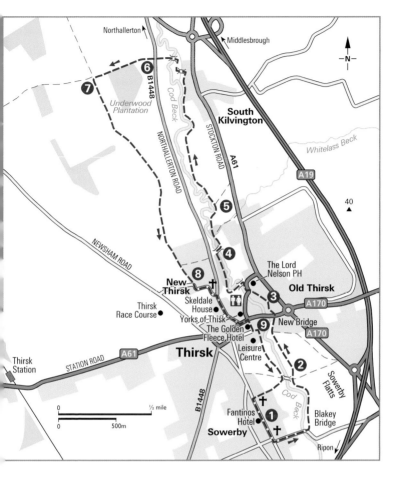

1. Walk down Front Street, away from Thirsk. Just past the Methodist church on the left, go left down Blakey Lane. Cross the bridge, turn left through a kissing gate and follow the stream, going through three more kissing gates to a footbridge.

2. Continue right of the stream to a stile. Go through two gates to a car park and ahead to the road. Cross and take a signed path that curves left, then right beside the bridge. At a paved area, turn right to go alongside a green to a road.

3. Cross the road and continue ahead, crossing a main road and going left at the top of St James' Green. Cross the metal bridge and continue beside the beck by the church. Before reaching the road, take the path to the right, beside benches, to a footbridge on the right.

4. Cross the bridge and go straight ahead through a gate, curving left by an electricity pole to follow the beck to a gate by a bridge. Go straight ahead (not over the bridge) and follow the path across the fields, veering diagonally right to a stile on your right.

5. Go over the stile and follow the stream, going over another two stiles to pass beside houses. Continue left over a footbridge by some mill buildings. The path winds right to cross a second footbridge. Go across the field through a gate opposite, and across a track to reach the main road.

6. Cross the road and go up a signed path opposite, to another gate. After 350yds (320m), turn left at a waymarker opposite a hedge at right-angles to the track.

7. Walk down the field with a hedge on your left. In the second field, bear left through a kissing gate and continue with the hedge on your right, bearing half left to another gate. Continue across the field, then down the next field-edges to a path that becomes a grassy lane between hedges.

8. At a road go straight ahead, bearing left, then right past the church. Turn right and walk into the town centre. On Market Place, cross by the clock tower towards The Golden Fleece. Go down a passageway, Roses Yard, two premises to the pub's left, cross a lane and go down Villa Place.

9. Bear left to pass the leisure centre. Turn right and bend round the building. Go ahead to a gate and straight ahead, parallel with the beck. At the bridge, turn right on a grassy track right of the hedge, to a gate onto a lane, then walk straight ahead back to Sowerby.

Where to eat and drink

Thirsk has a good choice of cafés, pubs and hotels. Recommended are the upmarket The Golden Fleece Hotel in Market Place and The Lord Nelson. Yorks of Thirsk, also in Market Place, offers good lunches and a range of coffees. In Sowerby, Fantinos Hotel offers tea and coffee all day, as well as dinner and Sunday lunch.

What to see

Catch a film at the Ritz Cinema, on Westgate, near Chapel Street. Built in 1912, it closed in 1992 when the economics of local cinemas had become almost impossible. The people of Thirsk were determined to have films back in their town, however, and, under the control of Thirsk Town Council, it was reopened in March 1995 and still shows a regular programme of films. It is now run entirely by volunteers. Its equipment – including a horn-shaped loudspeaker above the screen dating from the 1930s – has been updated, but the Ritz still retains the atmosphere of a typical small-town cinema of the past.

While you're there

Visit the Thirsk Museum at 14 Kirkgate and the tourist information centre on 93a Market Place. As well as having interesting local displays, this was the birthplace, in November 1756, of Thomas Lord. The son of a local farmer, Thomas made his name as a professional cricketer, and set up his own ground in Dorset Square, London, in 1787. Lord's Cricket Ground moved to its present site in 1814.

AROUND FOUNTAINS ABBEY

DISTANCE/TIME	6.75 miles (10.9km) / 3hrs
ASCENT/GRADIENT	687ft (204m) / ▲
PATHS	Field paths and tracks, some road walking, 2 stiles
LANDSCAPE	Farmland and woodland
SUGGESTED MAP	OS Explorer 298 Nidderdale
START/FINISH	Grid reference: SE270681
DOG FRIENDLINESS	Dogs should be on leads on field paths
PARKING	West Gate car park or at visitor centre, both National Trust
PUBLIC TOILETS	Fountains Abbey visitor centre

After you have climbed the hill from the car park and begun the walk along the valley side, following the ancient abbey wall, the south front of Fountains Hall is below you. Built by Sir Stephen Proctor in 1611, it is a fine Jacobean house with lots of mullioned windows and cross gables. Were it anywhere other than at the entrance to Fountains Abbey, it would be seen as one of the great houses of the age. Sir Stephen was, by all accounts, not the most scrupulous of men, having made his huge fortune as Collector of Fines on Penal Statutes. Nor did he respect the abbey buildings; the stone he built his house with was taken from the southeast corner of the monastic remains.

Abbey and abbot

A little further along the path, the abbey ruins come into view. When monks from St Mary's Abbey in York first settled here in 1132, it was a wild and desolate place. Nevertheless their abbey prospered, and became one of the country's richest and most powerful Cistercian monasteries. More remains of Fountains than of any other abbey ruin in the country. Its church was 360ft (110m) long. The other buildings, laid out along (and over) the River Skell, give a vivid impression of what life was like here in the Middle Ages. All came to an end in 1539 when King Henry VIII dissolved the larger monasteries. This was only a few years after Abbot Marmaduke Huby had built the huge tower, a symbol of what he believed was the enduring power of his abbey.

Mr Aislabie's garden

Beyond Fountains Abbey is the Water Garden laid out between 1716 and 1781 by John Aislabie and his son William. It is one of the great gardens of Europe, contrasting green lawn with stretches of water, both formal and informal. Carefully placed in the landscape are ornamental buildings, from classical temples to Gothic towers. The Aislabie mansion stood at the north end of the park; it was destroyed by fire in 1945. The highlight of the southern end of the walk is Markenfield Hall, a rare early 14th-century fortified manor house, built around 1310 for the Markenfield family. You can see the tomb of Sir Thomas

Markenfield and his wife Dionisia in Ripon Cathedral. Open only for booked tours, the house shows how a medieval knight and his family lived; it is part home, part farm. You can see the chapel and the great hall. The gatehouse, convincingly medieval, is 200 years younger than the house.

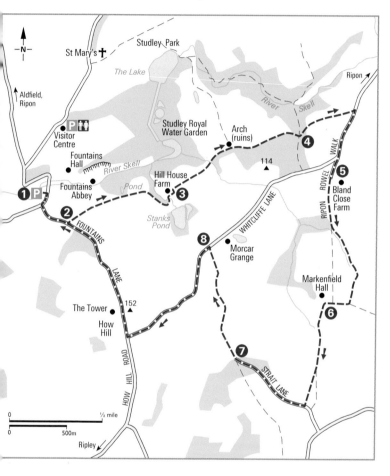

1. From West Gate car park turn right uphill, signed 'Harrogate'. At the fork go left, signed 'Markington, Harrogate'. Just after the road bends right, go left at a bridleway sign through a gate.

2. Follow the grassy path just inside the ancient abbey wall, past a small pond. Go through a waymarked gate and follow the track as it curves round to the right through another gate, then bend left to a gate into Hill House Farm.

3. Turn right then follow the bridleway signs to go left at the end of a large shed and then right. Go through a metal gate onto a track. At the end of the hedge go ahead down the field to a gate into the wood. Follow the track, passing a ruined archway, to descend to a crossroads of tracks.

4. Go straight across. The track climbs to a gate with a bridleway sign. Follow the track beside the line of trees to a gate onto Whitcliffe Lane. Turn right. At the top of the rise go straight ahead on the metalled road.

5. Go over the cattle grid by Bland Close Farm, then leave the lane to go straight ahead with the hedge on your right to a gateway. Continue through a gate along the waymarked track, eventually with woodland to your right. Follow the park wall through a gateway to reach a gate onto a lane. Turn right to reach some farm buildings by Markenfield Hall.

6. Follow the wall to the left, and bend left to go through a waymarked metal gate and straight ahead down the track, over a stile by a gate. Follow the track, then a waymarker sign, across a field to a stile by a gate. Turn right up the narrow Strait Lane, to emerge into a field.

7. Follow the waymarked path beside the hedge. Go through a gate in the field corner and continue ahead with the hedge to the right. After the next gate, bear half right to go through another gate. After the next field, do not go through, but bend left through a hedge gap and down the field side, with the hedge on your right, to go through a gate onto Whitcliffe Lane.

8. Turn left and follow the lane, which leads in the direction of How Hill Tower, an 18th-century folly, to a T-junction. Turn right here and follow the road back to the car park.

Where to eat and drink

The National Trust's visitor centre has a pleasant, airy restaurant offering snacks and meals. There is also a café at the east end of the Water Garden near the lake. Nearby Ripon offers a wider choice of pubs, restaurants and tea rooms.

What to see

Clearly visible from much of the walk is the spire of St Mary's Church in Studley Park. Now in the care of English Heritage, it was designed for the 1st Marquess of Ripon by the Victorian architect William Burges, between 1871 and 1878, at a cost of £15,000. It was money well spent. Where the exterior is restrained, the interior glows with colour and imagery. A dome over the altar is painted with angels. A carved, winged lion peers from the arches in the chancel. Mosaics show the heavenly city in the flooring. A brass door has a statue of the Virgin and Child. Burges's decoration gets richer from west to east, but throughout the church there is glowing, colourful stained glass. Even the organ seems to be trying to make a statement. In a corner of the south aisle is the alabaster tomb of the Marquess and his wife.

While you're there

As well as visiting the abbey and the garden, take the time to visit nearby Ripon. Its cathedral has a Saxon crypt, and in the stately market place is Britain's oldest free-standing obelisk, designed in 1702 by Nicholas Hawksmoor. You can discover Ripon's links with Lewis Carroll and how it inspired his Alice books, and see how the law was administered and the wicked punished on the Law and Order Trail.

20 LOFTHOUSE, RAMSGILL AND MIDDLESMOOR

DISTANCE/TIME	7 miles (11.3km) / 3hrs
ASCENT/GRADIENT	1,661ft (506m) / ▲
PATHS	Mostly field paths and tracks, may be muddy, 18 stiles
LANDSCAPE	Rich farmland and moorland, wide views from Middlesmoor
SUGGESTED MAP	OS Explorer 298 Nidderdale
START/FINISH	Grid reference: SE101734
DOG FRIENDLINESS	Can be off leads on walled section between Studfold Farm and Stean, but should be on lead for rest of walk
PARKING	Car park by Memorial Hall in Lofthouse
PUBLIC TOILETS	In Lofthouse

Much of upper Nidderdale was proposed as an Area of Outstanding Natural Beauty in 1947 – but official designation happened only in 1994, separately from the Yorkshire Dales National Park. It is an area of moorland wildness and deep, farmed valleys. In the late 19th and 20th centuries, parts of the dale were dammed as a chain of reservoirs – Angram, Scar House and Gouthwaite – was constructed to supply water to Bradford.

Monks, fairies and a murderer

Throughout Nidderdale are small, stone-built settlements like those visited on the walk – many of them of considerable antiquity. The monks of Fountains Abbey, near Ripon, founded the attractive village of Lofthouse as a grange in the Middle Ages. It was one of the bases from which they controlled their vast farming interests in Nidderdale. Ramsgill, at the southern end of the route, is at the head of Gouthwaite Reservoir, which is renowned for its spectacular bird life. The village was the birthplace, in 1704, of Eugene Aram, who arranged for the murder of his wife's lover and was hanged in Knaresborough for the crime – a deed retold by both Bulwer Lytton and the poet Thomas Hood. The village was also used in the film *Fairy Tale: A True Story* (1997) about two Yorkshire girls who hoaxed many – including Arthur Conan Doyle and Harry Houdini – into believing they had photographed fairies. In the third village, Middlesmoor, with its spectacular hilltop setting, the head of an Anglo-Saxon cross with its inscription to St Cedd in the church indicates the age of a settlement which today seems to date mainly from the last two centuries.

It was once possible to travel from Pateley Bridge up the dale on Britain's only corporation-run light railway. The Nidd Valley Light Railway ran regular passenger services from Pateley Bridge to Lofthouse, with stations at Wath and what was called Ramsgill (but was really at Bouthwaite). It closed to passengers in 1929, but the track is still visible on much of the route.

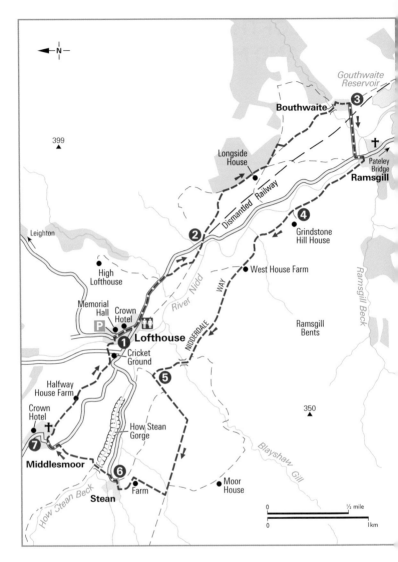

1. Walk downhill past the Crown Hotel. At the main road turn left. Just after the track to High Lofthouse farm go right, through a gate. Follow a clear track bending left to a waymarked stile, then bear left to another stile. Continue down to a slightly raised track (the old railway) and bear left to rejoin the road.

2. Cross the road and go through a gate, signed 'Bouthwaite'. Bear left off the farm track to a stile and ascend a grassy ramp. Bear left to climb more steeply, then right towards a plantation. Follow a clear path just below the plantation. Pass a house then join a track and follow it past a gate and Nidderdale Way sign to a fork. Bear left, still parallel to the plantation, then turn right over a stile. Descend left of a farmhouse, then bear left to a tall ladder stile. Walk straight ahead, keep a wall to your right and descend into a wooded valley.

Ignore a stile on the right and go through a waymarked gate, over a wooden bridge, through a metal gate and ahead. Bear right past a house down a gravelled track to a lane.

3. Turn right down the lane to a T-junction. Turn left, over the bridge. Turn right by the triangular green, then right gain, signed 'Stean'. Follow the track until it bends left up to Grindstone Hill House.

4. Go straight on, over four stiles. At West House Farm go over a stile between the farm and a bungalow, cross the farm road, follow waymarked posts (Nidderdale Way) and continue along a track, eventually descending to a signpost near a barn. Follow the obvious track into a valley and over a bridge.

5. At a T-junction of tracks, turn left. Follow the walled track uphill, bending right. As the main track bends left to Moor House, keep straight on along a grassy track. Another track joins from the left. Just beyond this, after crossing a stream, turn right. Bend left by a farm and then follow the track over a ford into Stean.

6. Follow the lane right, then take a stile on the left signed 'Middlesmoor'. Descend into How Stean Gorge, down steps, over a bridge and up steps, then follow signs to the road. Turn left into Middlesmoor. Turn right beside the Wesleyan chapel to the gateway of the parish church.

7. Turn right before the gate, through a stile signed 'Lofthouse'. Follow the path to Halfway House farm. Go through the farmyard to a gate and follow the right side of two fields, then bear left across the third to a gate in the corner. In the lay-by go left through a gate, then along the path beside the cricket ground. Cross the lane and go over a bridge, then bear right to emerge near the Market Cross in Lofthouse. Turn left to the car park.

Where to eat and drink
There are two Crown Hotels on or near the route, one in Lofthouse and another in Middlesmoor. Both serve food throughout the day.

What to see
The species of oil beetle, *meloë proscarabaeus*, has been sighted at Middlesmoor. Unlike other beetles, oil beetles' wing cases do not overlap, making them look as if they are wearing waistcoats. They also have kinked antennae – the male beetle's end with blobs. Oil beetles get their name from an oily fluid they secrete from their leg joints if they're disturbed. It deters predators and can cause blistering on human skin.

While you're there
The attractive town of Pateley Bridge has many fascinating small shops, as well as walks by the River Nidd and the interesting Nidderdale Museum in King Street, housed in a former workhouse.

SCAR HOUSE AND NIDDERDALE

DISTANCE/TIME	9.3 miles (15km) / 3hrs 45min
ASCENT/GRADIENT	2,146ft (654m) / ▲ ▲
PATHS	Moorland tracks, field paths and lanes, 13 stiles
LANDSCAPE	High hills of Upper Nidderdale, farmland and riverside
SUGGESTED MAP	OS Explorer 298 Nidderdale
START/FINISH	Grid reference: SE070766
DOG FRIENDLINESS	On leads on farmland; dogs are not permitted on access land between points 1 and 3
PARKING	Signed car park at top of reservoir access road
PUBLIC TOILETS	By car park at the start and in Lofthouse

Opened in 1936, Scar House is one of a string of reservoirs in Nidderdale that serve the city of Bradford, 30 miles (48km) to the south – the others include Angram, to the west, and Gouthwaite, down the valley towards Pateley Bridge. There is still evidence around the dam of the remains of the village in which the navvies who built it lived and of the ancillary buildings where they stored machinery and dressed the stone. There were some protests before the dams were built about the drowning of parts of the valley, and rumours that Nidderdale was left out of the Yorkshire Dales National Park when it was designated in 1954 because the reservoirs had blighted the landscape. Redress was made in 1994 when 603sq miles (1,562sq km) of Nidderdale was declared an Area of Outstanding Natural Beauty.

How Stean Gorge

'Yorkshire's Little Switzerland', says the publicity for How Stean Gorge. The How Stean Beck forced its way through the limestone, cutting a gorge up to 80ft (24m) deep, with pools and overhangs enough to please both geologists and small children. For a fee you can enter the gorge, crossing by footbridges and exploring the narrow paths. The more adventurous can borrow a torch to investigate the deep Tom Taylor's Cave, said to be named after a highwayman who holed up here.

The village of Middlesmoor, visible after passing How Stean Gorge, is one of the most dramatically sited in the area. Set high on a bluff overlooking the Nidd Valley, its 19th-century church is on the site of a building thought to have been founded by St Chad; it contains the head of a Saxon cross.

Following the Nidderdale Way from Lofthouse, you may see groups preparing to enter the Goyden Pot system, 3.5 miles (5.7km) of underground caves and passages cut by the River Nidd. An early guidebook noted that 'Goyden Pot Hole is a large Rock, into which the River Nidd enters by an arch finely formed & with a lighted candle a person may walk three hundred yards into it with safety'. This procedure is not recommended today!

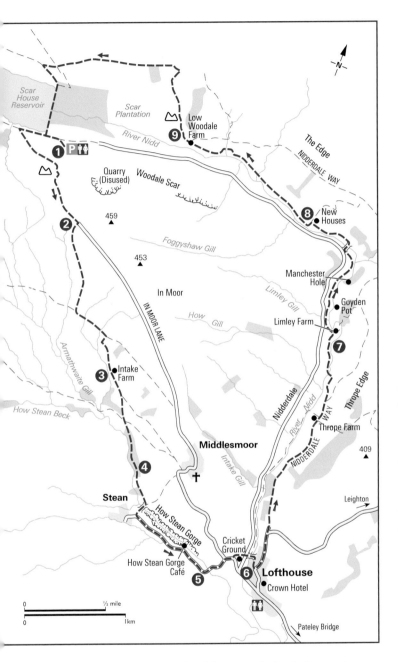

1. Walk past the dam and along the side of the reservoir. Just before a gate turn sharp left. The stony track climbs below crags then zig-zags up to open moor. Continue to a gate. A few paces beyond, go right through another gate.

2. Follow a path down to a wall and bear left. The undefined path goes through heather, roughly parallel to the wall, to a track. Turn left, cross two cattle

grids, then turn right, down to a gate. Walk down the field to a gate just right of a house.

3. Descend to a gate left of a ruined barn. Bear right through a gateway, then bear left through another gate to pass right of another barn. Continue in the same direction into woodland. A clearer path joins from the right; bear right, slanting down to the riverside.

4. Follow the path above the river, then through fields to a ladder stile and follow the edge of woodland to a gate and Nidderdale Way sign. Turn right down steps to cross a footbridge over the river. Follow the path to a lane and go left, passing How Stean Gorge entrance, to a stone bridge.

5. Follow the lane over the bridge to a T-junction and turn right. At a lay-by on a bend go through a kissing gate. Follow the path beside a cricket ground. Cross a lane and go over a bridge. Bear right and then pass between buildings to Lofthouse.

6. Turn left uphill. As the road bends right, go left on a level grassy track, signed 'Scar House Res'. Ignore branches to the right and follow the main track through five gates to Thrope Farm. Keep straight ahead through two more gates until a waymarked sunken path slants down to the river. Cross to a waymarked gate. Follow a path above the river, going over a stile in the fence on your right, then join a track towards a farm.

7. Pass metal sheds, then bear left to a metal gate beside a house. Follow the track to the riverbank and continue upstream. Eventually you will reach a footbridge over the river. Cross, go over the stile, turn left and continue along the riverside. At New Houses go through a gate, cross a lane and continue along the riverside track.

8. Where the track bends right, go ahead through three stone stiles and continue to a wooden stile. Climb slightly, then bear left to a gate. Descend to another gate, then bear right to a farm. Go ahead through two gates between the buildings to a track which climbs and bends right to pass another house.

9. Climb to a gap between high walls. Continue uphill, with a broken wall on your right, to a gate. Turn right. At a crossing track turn left, uphill, and follow the track until it crosses another track, directly above the dam. Descend to the dam and cross it to return to the car park.

Where to eat and drink

The Crown Hotel in Lofthouse does substantial bar meals at lunchtime and in the evenings, and serves good Yorkshire beer. The How Stean Gorge Café has a very good local reputation and an extensive menu.

What to see

The red kite, once a familiar sight all over England, was hunted almost to extinction in the 19th century. It has now been reintroduced in Yorkshire, and the birds have been seen over-wintering in Upper Nidderdale. They have flown in from their nesting sites on the Harewood Estate, near Leeds, or from Scotland.

22 ARNCLIFFE AND LITTONDALE

DISTANCE/TIME	6.5 miles (10.4km) / 3hrs 30min
ASCENT/GRADIENT	1,910ft (582m) / ▲ ▲ ▲
PATHS	Mostly clear, some rocky sections, may be muddy, 16 stiles
LANDSCAPE	Rocky hillside, moorland and meadows
SUGGESTED MAP	OS Explorer OL2 Yorkshire Dales - Southern & Western Areas
START/FINISH	Grid reference: SD932719
DOG FRIENDLINESS	On leads – sheep in fields and on moorland
PARKING	In Arncliffe, roadside parking in village
PUBLIC TOILETS	In Kettlewell

The village of Arncliffe may look familiar to long-time *Emmerdale* fans, for the opening titles for many years featured views of the village, and in the programme's early days it was used as a film location. The cameras have long departed, leaving visitors space to appreciate Arncliffe's spectacular setting. Great limestone scars – once home to the eagles who gave the village its name – line the hillsides all around, and the fells are riddled with caves and gulleys. Arncliffe sits on a great spit of gravel, above the floodplain of the River Skirfare. Before the bridge, a ford allowed travellers an easy crossing for the many ancient tracks that converge here. Some of the tracks may be prehistoric; there is evidence of Celtic field systems and stone enclosures.

An ancient village and thriving nature

St Oswald's Church may have been Saxon in origin, but nothing remains of that or its Norman successor. The tower is 15th-century, while the rest was rebuilt in the 18th and 19th centuries. The village records stretch back a long way however; the church retains a list of 34 men from the parish who went north in 1513 to fight the Scots at the Battle of Flodden. In Bridge House, close by, Charles Kingsley wrote part of *The Water Babies* – his Vendale is Littondale.

Arncliffe's houses, built of local stone, are set informally around the church and the green. There is some suggestion that it may have been initially a planned village, set here by monks who were clearing people off the surrounding land so that farming could be carried out more profitably.

Leaving Arncliffe, you will almost immediately begin the long climb up the hillside to Park Scar. The path passes through a patch of ancient woodland, Byre Bank Wood, which has regenerated itself with little management or felling for centuries, because of its precarious foothold on a steep bank. The descent to Kettlewell takes you through The Slit, a narrow cleft in the limestone rocks above the village, while the approach to Hawkswick gives views over Littondale, much of which is a conservation area. The fields are managed as wildflower meadows – look out for curlews, peregrine falcons and redshanks, as well as dippers, oystercatchers and yellow wagtails.

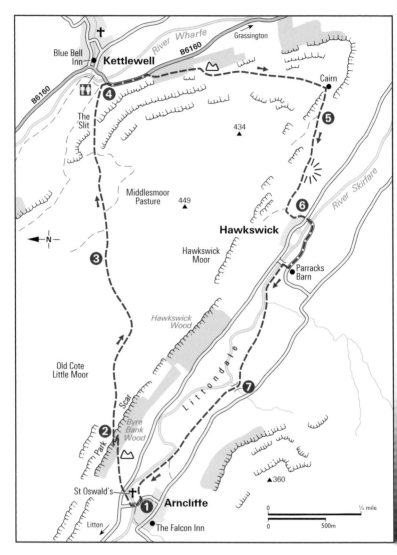

1. From outside the church, cross the bridge and turn immediately right, over a gated stile. Walk parallel with the river, cross the road via two stiles, then bear right and follow the footpath uphill over a stile and through a gate. Continue up in the same direction through the woods of Park Scar, with one short zig-zag near the top, to a stile.

2. Bear right and follow the footpath to another stile. Keep the same heading to pass a signpost, a tumbled wall and then another signpost. The path bears left, crosses a line of shakeholes and continues via a stile to another stile on the ridge.

3. Descend on the same heading. The path passes more shakeholes and descends beside a wall to a ladder stile. Follow the path down, descending steeply to a signpost. Cross a track and reach another signpost above a limestone scar overlooking Kettlewell. Descend a narrow cleft (The Slit), then descend to a track. Turn right and walk to the road (B6160).

4. Turn right for 300yds (274m), then go right through a gate by a fingerpost, bearing right again at another sign. Climb through woodland, go through a gate, then bear right and up to a small ruin. Continue along the edge of trees and round to a gateway beside a stile. Bear left to another stile then ascend the grassy path, keeping right where it forks, along a broad shelf. Eventually reach another stile and begin to descend, bending right by a cairn.

5. At a track junction continue ahead, with a wall on your left. The track leads down into Hawkswick village. On the outskirts go left, curve right between buildings and descend to the lane.

6. Cross the bridge and follow the lane round right. Just before farm buildings on the left, turn right towards a footbridge; turn left before it at the 'Arncliffe' sign. Follow the river to a footbridge over a side-stream and continue to a double gate. The path bears slightly away from the river to a gate. Cross the field beyond, skirting a steep bank above the river, to another footbridge.

7. Walk past a barn and through a gate, then bear left to a squeeze stile and cross a track. From the next stile bear slightly right to rejoin the river. Follow the path, with plentiful waymarkers and signs, to emerge by the churchyard and return to the start point.

Where to eat and drink

The Falcon Inn in Arncliffe has been run by the same family for four generations. Here you'll be served good beer direct from the barrel. There are no pumps; pot jugs are filled at the barrel and the ale is poured from them into your glass. They also serve home-cooked food.

What to see

The ancient village of Kettlewell's name means 'the stream in a narrow valley' – the village is built alongside the Dowber Gill Beck as it tumbles into the River Wharfe. Towering over Kettlewell are the long ridges of limestone and the huge bulk of Great Whernside. A weekly market used to be held at Kettlewell, which was on one of the main coaching routes from London to the North – beyond the village the route went over into Coverdale and into Richmond.

While you're there

The village of Litton is further up Littondale where the valley narrows, while beyond is the hamlet of Halton Gill. An 18th-century curate here, the Revd Miles Wilson, wrote a book to explain astronomy to ordinary folk. In *The Man in the Moon*, he imagines a cobbler climbing to the moon from the top of Pen-y-ghent, then wandering around exploring the solar system.

INGLETON AND ITS WATERFALLS

DISTANCE/TIME	5 miles (8km) / 2hrs 15min
ASCENT/GRADIENT	1,738ft (530m) / ▲ ▲
PATHS	Good paths and tracks, with some steps throughout
LANDSCAPE	Two wooded valleys, waterfalls, ancient track, wide views
SUGGESTED MAP	OS Explorer OL2 Yorkshire Dales – Southern & Western Areas
START/FINISH	Grid reference: SD69733
DOG FRIENDLINESS	Dogs should be on leads
PARKING	Pay-and-display car park in centre of Ingleton; limited parking at start of Waterfalls Walk
PUBLIC TOILETS	Ingleton
NOTES	Admission charge for Waterfalls Walk

This is one of the classic walks of the Yorkshire Dales, and was first opened to visitors in 1885. A workaday town, and today one of the Dales' honeypots, Ingleton shows its mining and quarrying history in its buildings. It became a place for tourists to visit when the railway arrived in 1859 – the viaduct almost cuts the village in half. The entrepreneurs who developed the Waterfalls Walk in the 1880s, and charged for the privilege of taking the route, were tapping into the start of one of the most profitable of industries in the Dales.

Cascades and strata

The spectacle of the Waterfalls Walk begins in Swilla Glen, where the River Twiss passes through a deep gorge, with rapids and whirlpools giving a taste of what is to come. The first of the cascades soon follows – Pecca Falls, where the river tumbles over a shelf of the hard greywacke stone, eating away at the softer slate beds below. Beyond, the narrow glen opens out as you approach Thornton Force. Unlike the other falls on the walk, this is not a series of rapids confined within the valley, but a majestic plunge of water 40ft (12m) from its lip of hard limestone into a pool gouged into the slate beds below, which have been heaved into a vertical position. This is a classic spot for studying the geology of the area; the different strata are conveniently exposed. A glacier came to this part of the valley – the tip of its nose reached just above the point where the water now falls. Here it deposited the mass of boulder clay it had pushed in front of it; the remains can still be made out beside the fall.

Limestone and water

The route beyond follows Twisleton Lane, an ancient packhorse route on the line of the Roman road from Bainbridge to Ingleton. Above you are Twisleton Scars, great bands of limestone interspersed with horizontal bands of shale. One of the best limestone pavements in the area is at the top of the Scars.

The walk then joins the second of the waterfall-filled valleys, this time of the River Doe. The woodland here is some of the oldest and most unspoiled in the area, with ancient oak trees flanking the waterfalls. Eventually the route leaves the river and comes out into a former limestone quarry – there is still quarrying in the area, for the greywacke, which is used for road surfacing.

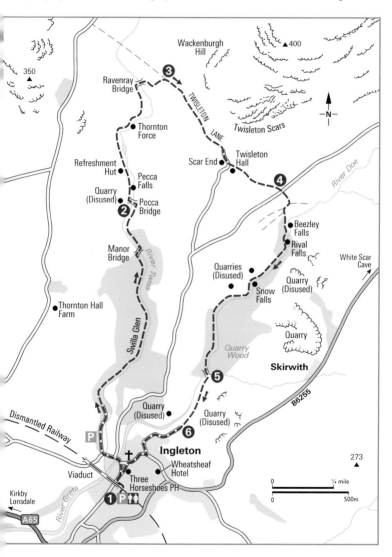

1. Leave the car park in the centre of Ingleton at its western end. Turn right along the road and follow the 'Waterfalls Walk' signs, which take you downhill and across the river to the entrance to the falls. Pay the admission fee, walk through the car park, and go through a kissing gate. The path undulates, with steps in places. Cross Manor Bridge and continue upstream, now with the river on your left, to Pecca Bridge.

2. Cross the bridge and turn right, continuing upstream and climbing to pass a refreshment hut before reaching Thornton Force. The path winds slightly away from the stream and up steps to pass the waterfall, and then takes you over Ravenray Bridge, and up more steps, to a kissing gate onto Twisleton Lane.

3. Turn right along the rough lane, where there's often an ice cream van. The track descends to a farmyard. Keep following 'Waterfalls Walk' signs through here, over a gated stone stile. Continue along the track, then though a kissing gate and onto a road.

4. Go straight across the road. The track soon bends right, passing a house. Go through a gate, then another into woodland. The path passes Beezley Falls and Rival Falls. A little further down, a side-path to the left leads to a footbridge with a good view of the deep and narrow Baxenghyll Gorge. Continue down the main path, which takes you to another footbridge.

5. Cross the bridge and follow the path past old slate workings, then away from the water into trees below the present-day quarry. The path eventually passes through the old limestone quarry workings. Continue through a hand gate onto a lane.

6. Beyond the gate follow the lane, soon entering Ingleton. Where the road divides, take the left fork to a T-junction and turn right. Follow the road round, passing the Three Horseshoes pub and just before the railway viaduct, steps on the left lead back up to the car park.

Where to eat and drink
Ingleton is well-served with places to eat and drink, among them Bernie's of Ingleton, the cavers' favourite, and Ingleton Chippy which serves traditional fish and chips. Among the pubs, the Wheatsheaf is highly recommended, while the Three Horseshoes specifically welcomes 'muddy boots and soggy dogs'.

What to see
Once growing in profusion in the area, the lady's slipper orchid is one of the rarest of Britain's endangered plants. They died out largely because of people digging them up to plant in their gardens, or taking them for their collections of pressed specimens. English Nature has now reintroduced this beautiful plant, which has large maroon-coloured flowers, with a yellow lip and red spots inside. Its leaves are pale green, with definite ribs to them. It is characteristic of open woodland, like that beside the waterfalls.

While you're there
A visit to White Scar Cave will take you underground into one of the country's largest caverns, discovered in 1923. An 80-minute guided tour passes underground waterfalls and gives you the chance to study the massive stalagmites and stalactites, some with names such as Devil's Tongue, Judge's Head and Arum Lily. The entrance is on the B6255, just north of Ingleton.

AUSTWICK AND THE NORBER ERRATICS

DISTANCE/TIME	5.25 miles (8.4km) / 2hrs 30min
ASCENT/GRADIENT	1,136ft (346m) / ▲ ▲
PATHS	Field and moorland paths, tracks, lanes, 8 stiles
LANDSCAPE	Farmland and limestone upland
SUGGESTED MAP	OS Explorer OL2 Yorkshire Dales – Southern & Western Areas
START/FINISH	Grid reference: SD769683
DOG FRIENDLINESS	Dogs should be on leads
PARKING	Roadside parking near Austwick Bridge and in village
PUBLIC TOILETS	None on route

There is nothing showy about Austwick village. A pleasant, grey-built village, it has several old cottages, many of them dated in the traditional Dales way by a decorative lintel above the main door, showing the initials of the couple who had it built, together with the year they moved in. They mostly date from around the end of the 17th century. On the green in the centre is the restored market cross. The market itself was lost centuries ago to nearby Clapham.

Robin Proctor and Nappa

The walk takes you up Town Head Lane from the village, and across fields into Thwaite Lane. To your left is the ridge of limestone called Robin Proctor's Scar, named after a local farmer whose horse was trained to bring him home after a long night spent in the local pub. One night, too drunk to tell, he mounted the wrong horse, and it plunged over the crag with the farmer on its back.

The area below the scar was formerly a tarn, and is now home to a wide variety of marsh plants. Nappa Scar, which the walk passes after you have visited the Norber Erratics, is on the North Craven Fault line. The path goes along a ledge below a steep cliff. In the cliff wall you can see the different strata of rock, including mixed conglomerate and limestone. To geologists they are a place of pilgrimage, and even the non-specialist can tell that something odd is going on here. When you arrive on the plateau above Nappa Scar you find an extensive grass-covered area, with the remnants of a limestone pavement poking through the tufts. Strewn all over the pavement are grey boulders, some of them huge, perched on limestone plinths. These are the erratics. Blocks of ancient greywacke stone, they were carried here from Crummackdale, more than half a mile (800m) away, by the power of a glacier, and dumped when the ice retreated. Over the centuries the elements have worn down the limestone pavement on which they stand – except where the erratics protected it, resulting in their elevated position.

After you cross Crummack Lane and walk though fields with a limestone ridge and ancient agricultural enclosures, you will reach Austwick Beck, where the water is crossed by an ancient clapper bridge – flat stones laid across the stream from bank to bank. This leads into a walled track to the hamlet of Wharfe. The route returns to Austwick along other walled lanes. These are the remains of old monastic ways that linked the granges, high on the fells, to the monasteries like Fountains Abbey which owned the vast sheep walks.

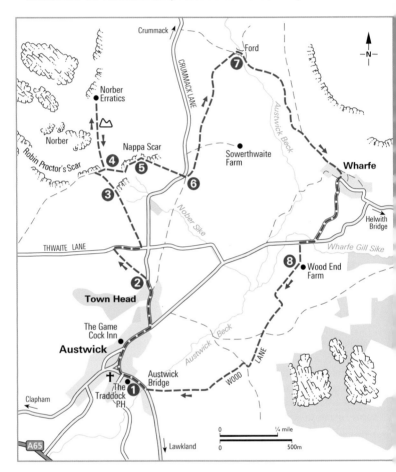

1. From the bridge, walk through the village. Bear right at the triangular green, following the signpost to Horton. Pass The Game Cock Inn and, just past a cottage called Hobbs Gate, turn left up Town Head Lane. Above the last of the houses, go left over a stone stile signed 'Clapham'.

2. Walk up the field to another stile, and on to a ladder stile onto a lane. Turn right. Just before reaching a metalled road, turn left over a ladder stile and follow a track. As the track veers left, go straight on, following the stone wall to a stone stile by a gate.

3. Cross the stile and continue up beside the wall. Where this bends left by a very large boulder across the path, go right on a track to pass the right-hand edge of the scar. When you reach a signpost, go up left, signposted 'Norber'.

4. Follow the path up onto the plateau and the Norber Erratics. Return the same way, back to the signpost. Turn left, following the sign for 'Crummack'. Follow the green path downhill then back up beside a wall by the scar to go over a stone stile on your right.

5. Descend to a gap by another stile and follow the path beneath a rocky outcrop. Continue downhill, with a wall on your left, to reach a gated stone stile onto a metalled lane. Cross the lane and go over another ladder stile opposite.

6. Turn left across the field. Go over two stone stiles, cross a farm track and go straight ahead on a slightly sunken grassy track over a rocky ridge to a stone stile. Continue to a gated stile, go left for a few paces and then right on a track. This soon leads to a ford and clapper bridge.

7. Cross over and follow the track between the walls for half a mile (800m) into Wharfe. Turn left at a T-junction in the hamlet, then follow the lane round to the right and go down to reach a metalled road. Turn right. After 100yds (91m), turn left at a bridleway sign to Feizor, down the road to Wood End Farm.

8. Turn right on a track beside the entrance to the farmyard. Follow it as it bends left and right, then bear right where another track joins from the left. Reaching a crossroads of tracks, take the middle of the three, towards a white-painted house. The track winds to reach the metalled lane into the village, a few paces from the bridge.

Where to eat and drink

The Game Cock Inn in Austwick is a traditional village pub with good ale and food and a great reputation. The Traddock, close to the start of the walk, is very much upmarket, with fine dining, as well as high-quality lunchtime snacks and cream teas.

What to see

Nothing is as characteristic of the Yorkshire Dales as its limestone scenery. It is technically known to geologists as a karst landscape – one that has underground drainage, with sinkholes and caves, dry valleys and limestone pavements like those above Crummackdale. Unlike most rocks, limestone is a soluble stone that is constantly being cleaned by the action of rainfall. Soils are not formed, plants do not appear, and the limestone remains pristine in its whiteness. But it is certainly not an unchanging landscape. The glaciers which originally scraped clean the limestone pavements have left their mark elsewhere, in the deep-gouged valleys and in the clefts where their meltwaters have torn through the rock. Even more spectacular are the caves under your feet, and the mysterious entrances to them. As you walk through this landscape, stalagmites and stalactite are still being formed beneath your feet.

While you're there

Clapham, to the northwest, which stole Austwick's market, is surrounded by attractive woodland. The village blacksmith at the end of the 18th century was James Faraday, father of the scientist Michael Faraday. From here, too, came the botanist Reginald Farrer, whose name appears in the Latin names of many of the plant species he discovered.

25 ALONG CATRIGG AND STAINFORTH

DISTANCE/TIME	5 miles (8km) / 2hrs 15min
ASCENT/GRADIENT	1,141ft (348m) / ▲ ▲ ▲
PATHS	Green lanes, field and riverside paths, some road, 8 stiles
LANDSCAPE	Moorland, farmland and river meadows with two waterfalls
SUGGESTED MAP	OS Explorer OL2 Yorkshire Dales - Southern & Western Areas
START/FINISH	Grid reference: SD821672
DOG FRIENDLINESS	Can be off lead in walled section up to Catrigg Force
PARKING	Pay-and-display car park in Stainforth, just off B6479
PUBLIC TOILETS	At car park

Stainforth is set along the Stainforth Beck as it rushes to join the River Ribble. It provides the starting point for many tracks across the moors to the east, once important routes for trade, that crossed the beck at first on the stone ford (which is what 'Stainforth' means) and later by the 14th-century bridge. The walk follows one of these ancient ways, the walled Goat Scar Lane, as far as the path down to Catrigg Force. This spectacular waterfall, hidden in a wooded valley, was one of the favourite places of the composer Edward Elgar, who regularly stayed with his friend Dr Charles Buck in nearby Settle.

Towards the end of the walk you pass another waterfall, Stainforth Force, where the Ribble passes over a series of limestone steps in tumultuous cascades. Just above is an attractive humpback bridge leading to Little Stainforth, a vital link on a packhorse route between Lancaster and Ripon.

Saving the pavement

After Catrigg Force, the walk route winds, after superb views towards Fountains Fell, towards the farms at Winskill. On the moorland just above are the Winskill Stones, pedestals of limestone topped with slate deposited here by ice age glaciers. The slate protected the limestone beneath from the erosion that has worn down the surrounding rock. An area of limestone pavement here is now a nature reserve, but was for many years quarried for ornamental garden rocks. After a campaign to prevent this destruction, 64 acres (26ha) was purchased from the owner for £200,000. Now the area, with its rare limestone plants, is preserved; it is dedicated to the memory of television gardener Geoff Hamilton, who was patron of the appeal that raised the funds to buy the land.

Sir Isaac Newton often came to Langcliffe Hall, which has an odd door surround probably carved by the same masons who worked on the much more elaborate house in Settle known as The Folly.

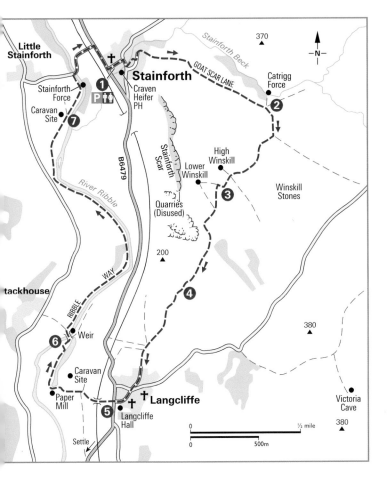

1. From the car park turn right, then right again, signed 'Settle'. Over the bridge, go immediately left through a gap in the wall. Follow the narrow path to an open area. Go through white posts and turn left. Keep right of the green, then turn right. Follow the track uphill for 0.75 miles (1.2km) to a gate. (To visit Catrigg Force, take a smaller gate to the left, then go left again. Return to the same point.)

2. After the gate, the track bends right. Go through another gate, then turn right, signed 'Winskill'. Join a track which bears left and runs between walls. At a signpost near the farmhouses, go straight ahead over a cattle grid and down a track signed 'Stainforth and Langcliffe'. Just after a right-hand bend, go left over a stile signed 'Langcliffe'.

3. Cross the field to a gate and stile, turning right immediately afterwards. The path soon descends steeply to a hand gate, bearing left just below to traverse the slope before descending to a gate. Follow the track beyond to another gate.

4. The track, now walled, leads into Langcliffe village. At a crossroads of tracks go a couple of paces right, then left (almost straight on). At the main street bear right, then keep straight on to reach the main road (B6479).

5. Cross the road to a gap in the wall diagonally right. Follow the footpath over a railway footbridge. Follow a lane ('No Entry' sign) towards a paper mill. Signs, barriers and fences guide the path round the works to emerge beside the millpond. Follow the pond-side path to reach a gate on the left by houses.

6. Go through the gate and turn right between the rows of cottages. Where the row ends, go left over a footbridge over the River Ribble and at the end turn right to a stone stile beside the weir, signed 'Stainforth'. Follow the riverside path for 0.75 miles (1.2km) before steps lead to a stile and an elevated stretch. The path returns gradually to the riverside and approaches a caravan site.

7. Go right of the site, on the riverside path, past Stainforth Force to the humpback Stainforth Bridge. Go through a stile onto the lane, turn right over the bridge and follow the narrow lane as it bends and climbs to the main road (B6479). Turn right and take the second turning left back to the car park.

Where to eat and drink
The Craven Heifer in Stainforth attracts visitors from far and wide – including King Charles III, who launched an initiative called 'The Pub is the Hub' here in December 2001 aimed at keeping village pubs open as a focus for the community. The pub serves traditional pub meals and offers a selection of made-to-order pies.

What to see
Stainforth Scar, seen from the riverside path in the latter part of the walk, is not a natural limestone cliff but the remains of a quarry, now being reclaimed by nature. More than 4 million tons of stone are quarried from the National Park each year, mainly for road building or for use in construction. Quarrying is a quandary in the Park. It provides local jobs in an area where they are scarce. Many of the permissions to quarry are long standing and have years to run – paying compensation is not an option. But conservationists argue that destroying an irreplaceable resource is not sensible, even though the companies make great efforts to clean up and plant trees as quarrying finishes. It is a complex problem, and will not easily be resolved.

While you're there
Visit Victoria Cave, east of Langcliffe. Nearly 1,500ft (457m) above sea level, the cave was discovered in 1838 (the year of Queen Victoria's coronation). Archaeologists revealed occupation by Roman, Celtic and Stone Age people, as well as animals – arctic foxes and reindeer – from the Ice Age and, in its earliest layers, hyenas and their prey, including elephants and woolly hippos.

MALHAM TARN AND MALHAM

DISTANCE/TIME	6.25 miles (10.1km) / 3hrs
ASCENT/GRADIENT	1,510ft (460m) / ▲ ▲
PATHS	Well-marked field and moorland paths, more than 400 steps in descent from Malham Cove, 5 stiles
LANDSCAPE	Spectacular limestone country, including Malham Cove
SUGGESTED MAP	OS Explorer OL2 Yorkshire Dales - Southern & Western Areas
START/FINISH	Grid reference: SD894658
DOG FRIENDLINESS	Mostly off leads, except where sheep are present or signs indicate otherwise
PARKING	At Water Sinks, near gateway across road
PUBLIC TOILETS	Car park in Malham village

As you begin this walk, the stream from Malham Tarn suddenly disappears in a tumble of rocks. This is the aptly named Water Sinks. In this spectacular limestone country, it is not unusual for streams to plunge underground but this particular stream has not always been so secretive. The now-dry valley of Watlowes just beyond Water Sinks was formed by water action. It was this stream, in fact, that produced Malham Cove, and once fell over its cliff in a waterfall 230ft (70m) high. Although in very wet weather the stream goes a little further than Water Sinks, it is 200 years since water reached the cove.

Pavement and cove
Beyond Watlowes valley you reach a stretch of limestone pavement – not the biggest, but probably the best-known example of this unusual phenomenon in the Dales. The natural fissures in the rock have been enlarged by millennia of rain and frost, forming the characteristic blocks, called clints, and the deep clefts, called grikes. Look closely into the grikes; their sheltered environment provides a home to spleenworts and ferns, and sometimes rare primulas. The limestone pavement is the summit of the most spectacular of natural features in the Yorkshire Dales – the huge sweep of the cliffs known as Malham Cove. Take care as you explore the pavement, as the edge is not fenced. As you descend the 400-plus steps, the sheer scale of the cove becomes apparent. It was formed by a combination of earth movement, glacial action and the biting away of its lip by the former waterfall.

Fields, falls and fairies
On the slopes to the east of Malham Cove you can see ancient terraced fields. Up to 200yds (183m) long, they were painstakingly cut and levelled by Anglian farmers in the 8th century for producing crops. They show how the population was expanding then – there was simply not enough farmland on the valley

floors to feed everyone. Beyond Malham village the route passes through fields and a wooded gorge – called Little Gordale – to Janet's Foss. One of the classic waterfalls of the Dales, it is noted for the screen of tufa, a soft, porous limestone curtain formed by deposits from the stream, which now lies over the original lip of stone that created the fall. Janet (or Jennett) was the queen of the local fairies, and is said to have lived in the cave behind the fall.

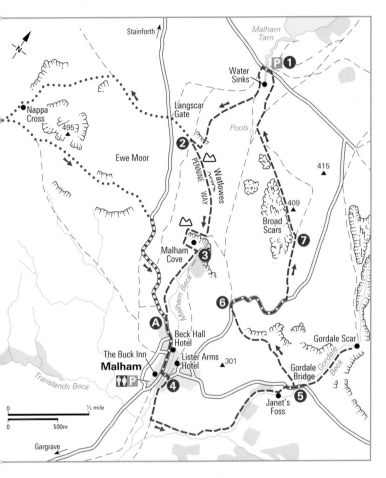

1. From the car park turn right onto the road and walk across the stream and then turn left through the kissing gate at the Malham Cove sign. Keep left at the next signpost, following the Pennine Way down the dry valley until the path bends sharp right, overlooking another dry valley.

2. Turn left, cross a stile and descend steeply into the lower valley. Walk down the level valley to a stile at the end. Just beyond this is the limestone pavement at the top of Malham Cove. Turn right and walk along the pavement. Take great care here, both of the sheer drop down to your left and the gaps in the limestone pavement (known as grikes). Turn left to descend beside a stone wall; go through a gate, then descend more than 400 steps to reach the foot of the cove.

3. At the bottom, fork left to visit the base of the cliff, then follow the obvious track beside the river. On reaching the road, turn left and follow it into the centre of Malham village. Turn left to cross the bridge.

4. Turn immediately right on a track past some houses, then continue along a gravelled path. Follow it left at a sign to Janet's Foss. Eventually the footpath enters woodland, then climbs beside a waterfall (Janet's Foss) to a kissing gate. Turn right along the road, towards Gordale Scar.

5. At Gordale Bridge (actually two bridges), go through a gate to the left. To visit Gordale Scar, continue straight ahead here. Take a signed gate to the left and follow the path through a field into the gorge. Continue as far as the waterfall and then follow the same route back to the bridge. On the main route, follow the signed public footpath uphill through three gates. Climb alongside a lane before emerging onto it.

6. Turn right and follow the lane uphill for 600yds (549m), to a ladder stile on the left. Follow a track to a footpath fingerpost.

7. Bear left and walk over a broad open moor before descending to some small pools. Turn right at the sign for Malham Tarn, go over a ladder stile, take the left-hand path and follow it back to the car park.

Extending the walk You can avoid the steep descent by Malham Cove by taking a scenic extension to this walk at Point 2, across the limestone uplands to Nappa Cross and descending to Malham along an old drove road which joins a minor road, rejoining the main route at Point A.

Where to eat and drink
As one of the most visited villages of the Yorkshire Dales, Malham is well-supplied with eating places. Beck Hall Hotel, the first you come to, has a riverside garden. The Buck Inn has good pub meals and fine beer. The Lister Arms Hotel has good food, real ale and, in summer, real cider.

What to see
Nothing is what is seems in the Alice-in-Wonderland world around Malham. The logical among us would assume that if water disappears underground, heading in the direction of Malham Cove just a mile (1.6km) ahead, it will reappear at the base of the Cove. But logic is wrong. The stream that bubbles up from under Malham Cove actually comes from Smelt Mill Sink, 0.75 miles (1.2km) to the west of Water Sinks. The stream from Water Sinks, on the other hand, reappears at Aire Head Springs to become the infant River Aire.

While you're there
Visit Gordale Scar (a short walk beyond Janet's Foss). The route takes you along a valley that rapidly narrows and twists beneath overhanging rocks, until a final bend brings you to the waterfall in the narrowest part of the gorge. Once thought to be a collapsed cave system, it is now believed to have been formed by erosion from the stream which has carved this spectacular gash through the limestone.

BORDLEY AND MASTILES LANE

DISTANCE/TIME	5 miles (8km) / 2hrs
ASCENT/GRADIENT	673ft (205m) / ▲
PATHS	Tracks and field paths, 2 stiles
LANDSCAPE	Moorland and farmland
SUGGESTED MAP	OS Explorer OL2 Yorkshire Dales - Southern & Western Areas
START/FINISH	Grid reference: SD952653
DOG FRIENDLINESS	On leads – sheep on moorland and livestock in fields
PARKING	Roadside parking on Malham Moor Lane, where lane reaches open moor
PUBLIC TOILETS	None on route

Many places in the Yorkshire Dales can be described as 'remote' but Bordley must be one of the least accessible. No metalled roads lead to it, and the settlement (a hamlet of a couple of farmhouses) is almost invisible, lying in a secluded hollow. Although the buildings are mostly 18th and 19th century, Bordley has a long, if uneventful, history. It is mentioned in Domesday Book as Borelaie, and its Old English name may mean 'the wood from which the boards were taken' – or perhaps 'the woodland clearing belonging to Brorda'. Whichever it is, the woods have long since gone, and this is now moorland country, some of it enclosed and improved in the 18th century for agriculture.

Around Bordley there is evidence of an even older settlement. Mastiles Lane ploughs through a Roman camp a little way to the west, while to the east, off the road up from Skirethorns, is evidence of a prehistoric field system.

Mastiles and the monks

The early part of the walk takes you to Mastiles Gate, a superb green track that for centuries has linked Wharfedale and Malhamdale. The monks of Fountains Abbey near Ripon needed easier access to their vast estates in the southern Yorkshire Dales and the Lake District. So, like the Romans before them, they constructed long roads directly over the fells. The route over Kilnsey Moor was marked by crosses – the bases of some survive. The monastic route crossed the River Wharfe by a wooden bridge at Kilnsey, and then went on to Ripon along the route of what is now the B6265 via Pateley Bridge.

In the 18th and 19th centuries Mastiles Lane was used as a drove road, when great herds of cattle were driven to market. There was a regular sale at Great Close, near Malham Tarn, where up to 5,000 cattle were regularly sold. It was at this time that the lane received its walls, to prevent the cattle straying.

Tarmac outcry

In the early 1960s plans were put forward to tarmac Mastiles Lane so that traffic would be able to drive from Malham into Wharfedale. A public outcry quickly saw the idea abandoned and the route is still a haven of peace for walkers and riders – though more recently there has been further controversy, this time about the use of such green lanes by four-wheel-drive off-road vehicles, which can cause damage.

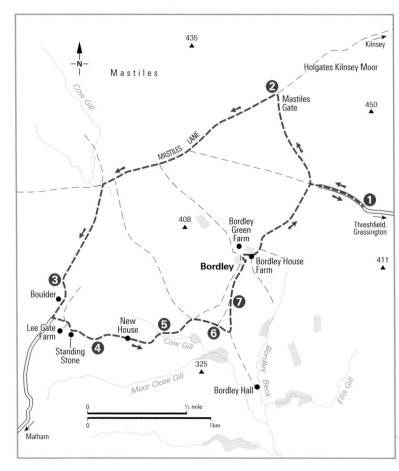

1. From the parking place, go through the gate and follow the metalled lane downhill to a crossroad of tracks. Turn right here, onto the track signposted 'Kilnsey'. Follow the track parallel with the dry-stone wall on your right to reach a crossing track at another signpost. This is Mastiles Gate.

2. Turn left along the lane signed 'Street Gate'. Follow the lane for 1 mile (1.6km), first climbing gently and then descending between walls into a shallow valley. Go through a gate and continue for about 100yds (91m) to a gate on the left from which a rough track heads down to ford a stream. Follow the rough track across the stream, over a slight rise and across rough pasture.

3. Eventually it runs between walls, bearing right near a large triangular boulder. Continue down to meet a metalled lane and turn left to Lee Gate Farm. Walk through the farmyard and over a cattle grid. Follow the farm track, crossing a cattle grid by a National Trust sign for New House farm.

4. Continue into a walled lane which leads into the farmyard of New House. Bear right through a gate then bear left down the field to a gate in the bottom left-hand corner. Go through the gate, turn left and follow the line of telegraph poles. Go over a stile and descend across the stream.

5. Climb away from the stream and bear right, then contour around the hillside. The path meets and follows a wall on your right. Go through the first gate on your right and follow the wall on your left, bearing right to go through a gap in the crossing wall.

6. Turn left to go round the angle of the wall on your left to a stone stile in the crossing wall. Follow the wall on the left up the field, past a tumbled wall, to join a track.

7. Turn right along the track and continue to a gate just above Bordley. Drop down right, then double back left to pass to the right of the first stone barn to double gates. Beyond the gates turn right and follow the track past the farmhouse. Climb the metalled lane, which reverts to rough track as it levels out. Descend to the crossroads and turn right to ascend the hill back to the start.

Where to eat and drink

Draw a circle of 4 miles (6.4km) in diameter centred on Bordley and you will not find a pub or café. So, before or after the walk, head for Grassington, which has plenty of tea shops as well as several recommended pubs including The Foresters Arms, or try the Old Hall Inn at Threshfield.

What to see

The merlin, Britain's smallest falcon, may sometimes be spotted above the moorland. The male has a blue-grey tail and back, while the larger female is brown-backed and has a banded tail. They most often nest on the ground, but have been known to occupy abandoned crows' nests. Like most falcons, their diet consists mainly of small mammals and insects, but more especially other birds, particularly ring ouzels and meadow pipits, which they catch in their swooping and spiralling flight.

While you're there

Visit Kilnsey Crag by the Wharfe where a great limestone cliff dominates the valley, with an overhanging nose that provides a severe test to climbers. The crag was formed when an Ice Age glacier ground away the end of a limestone spur as it made its way south from Littondale. Once, a lake lapped the crag's foot – it silted up long ago, leaving rich farmland.

THE MINES OF GREENHOW AND BEWERLEY MOOR

DISTANCE/TIME	6.5 miles (10.4km) / 3hrs
ASCENT/GRADIENT	1,467ft (447m) / ▲ ▲
PATHS	Field and moorland paths and tracks, 4 stiles
LANDSCAPE	Moorland and valley, remains of lead-mining industry
SUGGESTED MAP	OS Explorer 298 Nidderdale
START/FINISH	Grid reference: SE128643
DOG FRIENDLINESS	Dogs can be off leads for much of route
PARKING	Car park at Toft Gate Lime Kiln
PUBLIC TOILETS	None on route

It is a long haul from Pateley Bridge up Greenhow Hill to the village of
Greenhow, one of the highest in Yorkshire at around 1,300ft (396m) above
sea level. Until the early 17th century this was bleak and barren moorland.
When lead mining on a significant scale developed in the area in the 1600s, a
settlement was established here, though most of the surviving buildings are
late 18th and 19th century. Many of the cottages have a small piece of attached
farmland, for the miners were also farmers, neither occupation alone giving
them a stable income or livelihood. In a way typical of such mining villages, the
church and the pub – The Miners Arms (now closed) – are at the very centre.

Romans and monks
Romans are the first known miners of Greenhow, though mining activity
may go as far back as the Bronze Age. The Romans had a camp near Pateley
Bridge, and ingots of lead – called 'pigs' – have been found nearby, dating from
the 1st century AD. In the Middle Ages, lead from Yorkshire became important
for roofing castles and cathedrals. Production was governed by the major
landowners, the monasteries; some, like Fountains and Byland, became rich
from selling charters for mining and from royalties. After the monasteries
were dissolved, the new landowners wanted to exploit their mineral rights, and
encouraged many small-scale enterprises in return for a share of the profits.

As you leave Greenhow and begin to descend into the valley of the Gill
Beck, you pass through the remains of the Cockhill Mine. It is still possible to
make out the dressing floor, where the lead ore was separated from the waste
rock and other minerals, and the location of the smelt works, where the ore
was processed. Beyond, by the Ashfold Side Beck, were the Merryfield Mines,
and where the route crosses the beck there are extensive remains of the
Prosperous Smelt Mill. All these mines were active in the middle of the
19th century, and some had a brief resurgence in the mid-20th century.

Besides the lead
The vast retaining banks of Coldstones Quarry rise above the car park at Toft
Gate Lime Kiln. You can view this enormous hole from Coldstones Cut (access

from the back of the car park); this huge public work of art by Andrew Sabin has two ascending spirals of stone walls either side of a central spine. Opened in 2010, it's worth the climb for the superb views from the top and to marvel at the quarry. Around Greenhow the limestone layers are particularly deep, allowing large blocks to be cut. Across it run two mineral veins, called Garnet Vein and Sun Vein, both of which have been mined for lead and for fluorite.

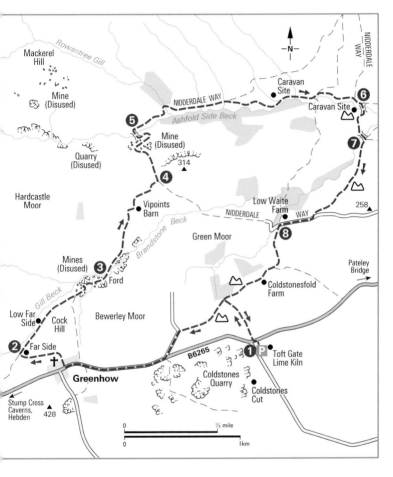

1. Cross the road from the car park and go over the stile beside a metal gate opposite into a field. Follow the faint path downhill to turn left just before a gate. Follow the wall on your right to a stile near a metal gate onto a metalled track. Turn left and walk up the hill to a metal gate onto a road. Turn left and walk up to the main road. Turn right and follow this down into Greenhow village. At the bottom of the hill, just past a converted chapel (Old Hall), take a lane signed 'Stripe Lane', to the right. At the junction go left and follow the lane to a cattle grid. Follow waymarkers along the wire fence to go through a gate on your right and bear round to the right to pass behind the house (Far Side).

2. Follow the track as it skirts the house and on past Low Far Side. Continue down into the valley of Gill Beck and then Brandstone Beck, where there are the extensive remains of lead mining activity. Follow the main track as it winds to the right of a building and across a ford.

3. Follow the track beside a ruined arch and up the hill. Go over a stile beside a gate by trees then, 100yds (91m) beyond, bear right through a gateway. Follow the track towards a house but before reaching it, turn left at a way-marker between stone walls and descend to a T-junction with another track.

4. Turn left, signed 'Ashfold Side'. Descend to spoil heaps, then leave the track to follow a steep path downhill just to the right of the heaps to a footbridge over Ashfold Side Beck.

5. Cross and follow the path to meet a track. Follow this down the valley, eventually going through a series of caravan sites. About one mile (1.6km) from the footbridge, the Nidderdale Way leaves the track at a Heathfield signpost. Go straight on for another 100yds (91m), then turn right through a metal gate by a Low Wood sign and then over a bridge.

6. Bear right up the steep track and, as the gradient eases, go left on a green track between stone walls. Nearing a house, bear right to cross a footbridge.

7. Turn right through a gate and follow the rough track uphill. Meet another track at a T-junction and turn left, but as the track begins to bend left, bear right across the grass to a kissing gate and a metalled lane. Turn right.

8. About 100yds (91m) after passing Low Waite Farm on the right, fork left on a track signed 'Toft Gate'. Just before a cattle grid turn right, go through a gate and follow the rougher track up to Coldstonesfold Farm. Continue along the metalled track. Just after the end of the metalled road go left over a stile to retrace your outward route to Toft Gate Lime Kiln.

Where to eat and drink
Either head west to Stump Cross Caverns and its tea room or east to Pateley Bridge. There are plenty of options in Pateley Bridge with several hotels, pubs, restaurants and tea rooms, including the Old Granary teashop.

What to see
The lime kiln at Toft Gate is very well-preserved and is now protected by English Heritage. It was built in the 1860s to help meet the Victorians' huge demand for lime, both in agriculture and building. A path from the car park leads you round the site where the flue, chimney and main furnace are visible. You can also see inside the kiln itself and interpretive panels explain the workings.

While you're there
The limestone cave system at nearby Stump Cross Caverns was discovered in the middle of the 19th century. You can visit a succession of caves with plenty of stalagmites and stalactites, many with fanciful names, where ancient animal bones have been discovered. It is open daily from mid-February to mid-November and winter weekends.

EXPLORING GISBURN FOREST

DISTANCE/TIME	3.25 miles (5.3km) / 1hr 30min
ASCENT/GRADIENT	439ft (113m) / ▲ ▲
PATHS	Forest tracks and footpaths
LANDSCAPE	Wooded valleys, forest, beckside heathland
SUGGESTED MAP	OS Explorer OL41 Forest of Bowland & Ribblesdale
START/FINISH	Grid reference: SD732565
DOG FRIENDLINESS	Fine for dogs under reasonable control
PARKING	Stocks Reservoir car park at Gisburn Forest
PUBLIC TOILETS	None on route

Perfectly placed between the Yorkshire Dales and the Forest of Bowland, Gisburn Forest in the Upper Hodder Valley is the setting for this short, circular stroll. You will walk along open, naturally wooded valleys, beside a tumbling beck and over heathland. You will have views over the reservoir and up to the fells, and you will hear the woodland birdsong and the call of the wildfowl on the water. If you're lucky, you may spot a deer, footprints in the sandy earth confirming their presence.

Stocks Reservoir

The two defining aspects of this walk are the open waters of Stocks Reservoir and the woodlands of Gisburn Forest. The reservoir was built in the 1930s to provide drinking water for the towns of central Lancashire. The village of Stocks was submerged in the process along with many ancient farmsteads. It was formed by damming the River Hodder and can hold 2.6 billion gallons (12 billion litres) of water when it is at full capacity. Attractively placed on the edge of the forest, the reservoir is an important site for wildfowl, and 30 different species visit during the winter, including red-throated divers, whooper swans, gadwalls and great crested grebes. Among the different birds of prey who frequent the area, ospreys and peregrine falcons have been spotted, as well as a rare passing marsh harrier. A bird-watching hide is provided, and a pleasant permissive footpath winds around the shoreline.

The Forestry Commission's extensive woodland known as Gisburn Forest was developed at the same time as the reservoir and was opened in 1932. It covers 3,000 acres (1,214ha), making it the largest single forested area in Lancashire. There are several waymarked trails to be enjoyed, and a cycle network extends to over 10 miles (16.1km). Although the majority of the plantations are of the monotonous coniferous variety and are managed principally as a commercial crop, more broadleaf trees are being planted to improve the visual aspect and to increase the diversity of wildlife. The forest and the reservoir are now managed in tandem, to develop a sustainable economic base for this beautiful landscape.

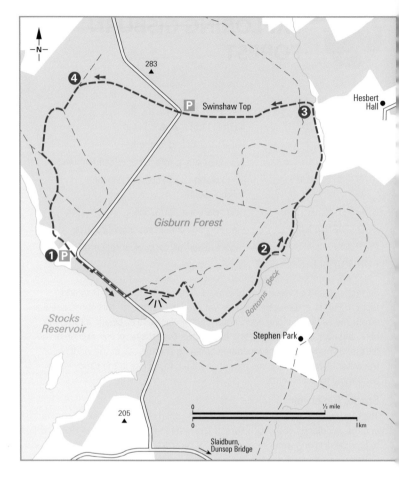

1. Leave Stocks Reservoir car park at the right of the two vehicular entrances. Follow a path right of the road until it bends away; cross the road and continue on it until you reach a broad forest track. Turn left; a red and blue marker post soon confirms your route. At the fork in the paths carry straight on. There are good views right, through the trees to the reservoir and causeway with the fells in the background. Keep on the track as it takes you beside open wooded valleys and through natural woodland with a river down on your right.

2. Pass a short track down to the right. Soon the main track forks; take the narrower right branch, through a sort of cutting, then bear right and down towards the river. The track soon divides but the two branches rejoin further on. The right branch runs close to the tumbling peaty Bottoms Beck, with fields rising to Hesbert Hall beyond it.

3. After the two branches of the paths merge again, two red marker posts in quick succession direct you sharply up and left on a rougher path, which is quite hidden. Meet a forest track, go a few paces right, then left again on a continuation path. Follow it gently uphill onto a log staircase, passing upright gateposts by a collapsed ruin. Walk through Swinshaw Top car park to the

road and go straight over to take a narrow footpath through the woods by another red marker post. The path opens onto a broadish green swathe but is soon closed in again; however, lovely elevated views over the reservoir to the left, and the fells ahead; make the start of your descent pleasurable.

4. Meet a forest track at a bend, proceed straight ahead (slightly right) and follow the track for 200yds (183m) until red posts turn you right, down a footpath with a stream on the right. At a T-junction of footpaths, turn left across open heathland on a clear path back to the car park.

Where to eat and drink
Nothing is available within the forest itself, so it might be an idea to pack a picnic. Alternatively, head 4.5 miles (7.2km) southwest to Slaidburn, where you'll find the popular Riverbank Tea Rooms (closed Mondays in winter). Just up the village street is the famous 13th-century Hark to Bounty pub, which serves good bar meals (open Thursday to Sunday).

What to see
It's more a case of what to listen for! The birdsong throughout the walk, from tiny wrens darting into the bushes to the cry of the curlew skyward, is symphonic. Add to that the call of the wildfowl on the reservoir, never far away, and the orchestration is complete.

While you're there
The Forest of Bowland is a designated Area of Outstanding Natural Beauty (AONB) occupying the northeastern corner of Lancashire. It is a landscape of barren gritstone fells, moorland and steep-sided valleys, with 3,260 acres (1,320ha) of open country available to walkers. The village of Dunsop Bridge in the Trough of Bowland claims to be the official centre of the country – a telephone box adjacent to the village green marks the precise spot.

THE LEEDS AND LIVERPOOL CANAL AT GARGRAVE

DISTANCE/TIME	3.5 miles (5.7km) / 1hr 30min
ASCENT/GRADIENT	279ft (85m) / ▲
PATHS	Field paths and tracks, then canal tow path, 2 stiles
LANDSCAPE	Farmland and canalside
SUGGESTED MAP	OS Explorer OL2 Yorkshire Dales – Southern & Western Areas
START/FINISH	Grid reference: SD931539
DOG FRIENDLINESS	Dogs should be on leads, except on the canal bank
PARKING	Car park near Village Hall, signed from A65
PUBLIC TOILETS	By bridge in Gargrave

Gargrave has long been a stopping-off point for travellers from the cities of West Yorkshire on their way to the coast at Morecambe or to the Lake District. These days, most of them arrive along the A65 from Skipton, the route formerly taken by horse-drawn coaches. There is still evidence of the village's importance as a coaching centre, especially at the Old Swan Inn. Its position beside the River Aire had also proved important when 18th- and 19th-century surveyors were seeking westward routes for other methods of transport. The walk crosses the railway not long after leaving Gargrave; this is the route that, not far west, becomes the famous Settle-to-Carlisle line. And you will return to the village beside the Leeds and Liverpool Canal.

Earlier settlers, mills and bandages
Although Gargrave is today mostly a 19th-century settlement, there is evidence that the area has been in occupation much longer. The site of a Roman villa has been identified nearby, while on West Street excavation has found the remains of a moated homestead dating from the 13th century, which was reused in the 15th century. By the 18th century there were cotton mills in Gargrave, served by the canal, and weavers were producing cloth for the clothing industry. Their expertise resulted in the establishment here of a big employer, Johnson and Johnson Medical, now Systagenix, as workers could undertake the fine weaving that was needed to produce bandages.

Canal digging
In October 1774, the eastern arm of the Leeds and Liverpool Canal, snaking its way westwards from Leeds, reached Gargrave. Work began at both the Liverpool and the Leeds ends, but there were, inevitably, arguments between the separate committees in Yorkshire and Lancashire about both the route and the finances. It was not until 1810 that the canal opened across the Pennines allowing barges to go from Leeds to Blackburn, and only in 1816 was the full distance of 127 miles (204km) open to Liverpool. Gargrave benefited not only

from the access it gave the village to the raw materials for the cotton mills and the chance to export its cloth, but also as a stopping place for the bargees. The walk joins the canal near the lowest of the six locks at Bank Newton, where the canal begins a serpentine course to gain height as it starts its trans-Pennine journey. Near the lock is the former canal company boatyard where boats for maintaining the canal were built. As you walk along the tow path you will cross the Priest Holme Aqueduct, where the canal is carried over the River Aire.

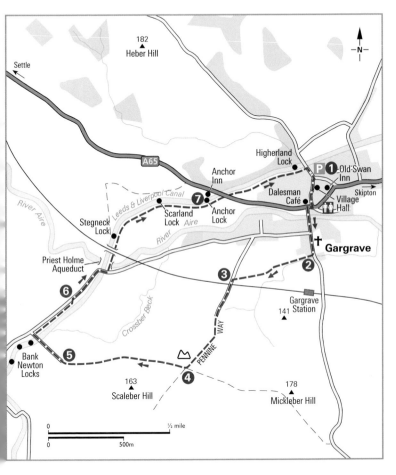

1. Walk down the lane past Gargrave Village Hall. At the main road (A65) turn right, cross the road and go left into Church Street and over the bridge. Pass the church on your left. Just past Church Close House on your right, turn right, following a Pennine Way sign. Go over a stone stile in the wall on your left.

2. Turn right along the wall, following the Pennine Way path, which is partly paved here. Go ahead across the field to a waymarked gate, then half left to another gate. Walk up the field, left of power lines, to a gate in the top left corner, which leads to a rough sunken lane.

3. Turn left over a railway bridge, then follow the track up a small hill. Cross a cattle grid, then leave the track to cross a stile on the left into a field. Take a faint path half right then join a track, making for a signpost on the skyline.

4. At the post, turn right to the corner of a wire fence, then slant down onto a grassy ramp to reach a waymarked gate in a crossing fence. Go ahead across the field to a pair of gates. Take the waymarked left-hand one and continue ahead, at first following a fence and line of trees. Continue straight ahead to meet a gate across a track.

5. Go through the gate and follow the track down to go through another gate to the canal by Bank Newton Locks. Cross the bridge and turn right along the tow path. Where the tow path runs out, join the lane which runs alongside the canal.

6. Go ahead along the lane, cross the bridge over the canal, then turn right through a gate down a spiral path to go under the bridge and continue along the tow path. Pass over a small aqueduct over the river, then under a railway bridge. Continue past Stegneck Lock and Scarland Lock to reach Anchor Lock.

7. Beyond the lock, opposite the Anchor Inn, go under the road bridge and continue along the tow path to reach Bridge 170, at Higherland Lock. Go onto the road by a signpost. Turn right down the road, back to the car park.

Where to eat and drink

Gargrave has several restaurants, tea shops and cafés. The Dalesman Café and Sweet Emporium is a Dales institution especially popular with cyclists. The Old Swan Inn on the A65 has meals at lunchtimes and in the evenings.

What to see

It's worth looking closely at the locks as you walk along the canalside. Bank Newton Locks and the others along this stretch of the canal have the usual paddles, operated by a crank-operated gear, to open the ground holes at the base of the lock gates. At Higherland Lock, however, reached just before you leave the canal, there is a much simpler method. Beside the gates there are apparently two more, rather badly made, gates. These are the barriers which protect the ground holes, and they are simply pushed aside to let the water through. Look out along the way, too, for the iron markers that detail the distance between Liverpool and Leeds, and the elegant iron signposts. The bridge by which you regain the tow path after a short section along the road is designed to enable the towing horse to change from one side of the canal to the other.

While you're there

Explore more canal history at nearby Skipton, where the Leeds and Liverpool Canal runs through the heart of the old town. You should also visit the fine parish church at the top of the High Street, and the nearby castle, with its splendid twin-towered gatehouse. Conduit Court, the heart of the castle, has a fine old yew tree in its centre.

BOLTON ABBEY AND THE STRID

DISTANCE/TIME	7 miles (11.3km) / 2hrs 30min
ASCENT/GRADIENT	1,716ft (523m) / ▲
PATHS	Field and moorland paths, then riverside tracks, 3 stiles
LANDSCAPE	Moorland with wide views and riverside woodland
SUGGESTED MAP	OS Explorer OL2 Yorkshire Dales – Southern & Western Areas
START/FINISH	Grid reference: SE071539
DOG FRIENDLINESS	Must be on leads in woodland and on moors
PARKING	Main pay-and-display car park at Bolton Abbey
PUBLIC TOILETS	By car park and at Cavendish Pavilion

Bolton Abbey has always been one of the showpieces of the Yorkshire Dales, and attracts many visitors, most of whom stay close to the monastic buildings or venture only to The Strid. This walk takes you a little further afield, and has the priory – it was never an abbey – as its climax.

After passing under the archway (in fact, an aqueduct built in the 18th century to carry water to a mill), you reach Bolton Hall. In part originally the gateway to Bolton Priory, this was later extended as a hunting lodge for the Earls of Cumberland and their successors the Dukes of Devonshire, who still own the estate. The wings are said to be by Sir Joseph Paxton, designer of the Crystal Palace. The walk then passes westwards through woodland to the top of a hill offering excellent views west towards the Aire Valley and north over Barden Fell.

The priory was built for Augustinian canons who founded their house here in 1154. The ruins make one of the most romantic scenes in the country, and all the great English artists, from Thomas Girtin and J M W Turner on, have painted it. Much of what remains was complete by 1220; the last prior, unaware of the oncoming storm that would sweep away monastic life, began a tower at the west end. It remained unfinished when the monasteries were suppressed. Most of the buildings fell into ruin, but the nave of the priory church was given to the local people, and it is still their parish church. A former rector, William Carr, spent 54 years here, laying out the paths along the valley that are now enjoyed by so many visitors.

The thundering Strid

At the entrance to the woodland around The Strid there are information boards that explain the birds and plants you can find here, including the sessile oak. Characteristic of the area, it is distinguished from the pedunculate oak by the fact that its acorns have no stalks. At The Strid itself the River Wharfe thunders through a narrow gorge between rocks. The underlying geology is gritstone, with large white quartz pebbles embedded in it. The Strid was a place loved by the Victorians, but the flow is fast and the river is 30ft (9m) deep here with strong eddy currents, so don't be tempted to cross; there have been many drownings here over the years.

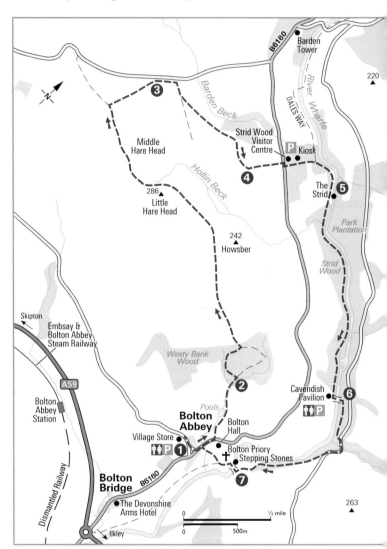

1. Leave the car park at its north end, by the Village Store. Turn right and walk to the B6160. Turn left and follow the road – taking care with oncoming traffic – under an archway. Opposite the battlemented Bolton Hall, turn left on a signed track. At the top of the track, go through a gate on the right with a bridleway sign. Walk towards the left under a power line to a signpost. Go past two pools, through a gate, then bear right to another gate into woodland.

2. Follow the rising track through the wood, with several signs, to another gate. Follow blue waymarkers, most painted on rocks, across fields. At a crest bear left to a gate in a corner, then turn left along the wall. The path climbs more steeply onto Hare Head, which has wide views. Descend gently to a gate, and 20yds (18m) beyond, take a path downhill, bearing right lower down to a signpost.

3. Turn right on a path parallel to the road, to another signpost 'FP to B6160'. Follow the track to a stile, then take the left fork, going roughly level across the moor, to a wall corner. Continue to the next wall, then turn right along it, following an improving track to a signpost.

4. Turn left over a stile and follow the wall down to the road. Turn right for a few paces then enter a car park. Pass beside the Strid Wood Visitor Centre and follow tracks, signed 'The Strid', down to reach the river close to its narrowest part at The Strid.

5. Follow the wide tracks downstream until you reach an information board and gateway near the Cavendish Pavilion. Bear left by the café and the cross the footbridge.

6. Immediately after the bridge turn right, marked as a permissive footpath, as part of The Dales Way. The path briefly joins a vehicle track to cross a side-stream then bears right. When the path forks, take either branch (the higher has better views of the priory). Descend to a bridge beside stepping-stones near the priory.

7. Cross the bridge and walk straight on. Climb steps to a gateway – the Hole in the Wall. Go through to the road, left a few paces, then right to return to the car park.

Where to eat and drink

Bolton Abbey has a couple of lovely cafés near the car park, and the Devonshire Arm Hotel, with its Brasserie and main Burlington restaurant, is south of the start. The Cavendish Pavilion has snacks, lights meals and afternoon teas.

What to see

Bolton Priory church is a mix of Norman and later styles. The west front is complicated – it has a huge decorative window, but masks an even better 13th-century west front. The eastern end of the church is in ruins but look for the remains of the huge east window. The nave, now the parish church, still conveys the building's original grandeur. The stained-glass windows on the right-hand side as you enter date from the first half of the 19th century and were designed, in convincing medieval style, by Augustus Pugin, whose decorative work is found in the Houses of Parliament.

While you're there

Take a trip on the Embsay and Bolton Abbey Steam Railway, which has a station 1.5 miles (2.4km) south of the Priory. Operated by enthusiasts, the railway runs steam trains at weekends, and on most days in August; at other times there is a historic diesel service.

A CIRCUIT OF ADDINGHAM AND ILKLEY

DISTANCE/TIME	5.5 miles (8.8km) / 2hrs
ASCENT/GRADIENT	527ft (160m) / ▲
PATHS	Riverside path and field paths, some road walking, several stiles
LANDSCAPE	Rolling country and the River Wharfe
SUGGESTED MAP	OS Explorer 297 Lower Wharfedale & Washburn Valley
START/FINISH	Grid reference: SE083498
DOG FRIENDLINESS	Not advised due to loose dogs at Low Austby Farm
PARKING	Lay-by at eastern end of Addingham, on bend where North Street becomes Bark Lane by information panel
PUBLIC TOILETS	On riverside near footbridge in Ilkley

Addingham's houses extend for a mile (1.6km) on either side of the main street, with St Peter's Church at the eastern end of the village. So it's no surprise that the village used to be known as 'Long Addingham', and that it combines three separate communities that grew as the textile trades expanded at the end of the 17th century. Within 50 years, Addingham's population quadrupled, from 500 to 2,000. At the height of the boom, there were six woollen mills in the village. Low Mill, built in 1787, was the scene of a riot by a band of Luddites – weavers and shearers who objected to their jobs being done by machines. Though the mill itself was demolished in 1972, more houses were added to the mill-hands' cottages to create Low Mill Village, a pleasant riverside community.

Elegant Ilkley

Ilkley is a town that seems to have more in common with Harrogate, its even posher neighbour to the north, than with the textile towns of West Yorkshire. The Romans established an important fort here – believed to be Olicana – on a site close to where the parish church is today. Two Roman altars were incorporated into the base of the church tower, and taken into the church for safekeeping are three Anglo-Saxon crosses from the 8th or 9th centuries. One of the few tangible remains of the Roman settlement is a short stretch of wall near the handsome Manor House, which is now a museum.

Like nearby Harrogate, Ilkley's commercial fortunes changed with the discovery of medicinal springs. During the reign of Queen Victoria, the great and the good would come here to 'take the waters' and socialise at the town's hydros and hotels. Visitor numbers increased with the coming of the railway, and, with its open-air swimming pool and riverside promenades, Ilkley was almost an inland resort. Ilkley remains a prosperous town, unashamedly dedicated to the good things of life.

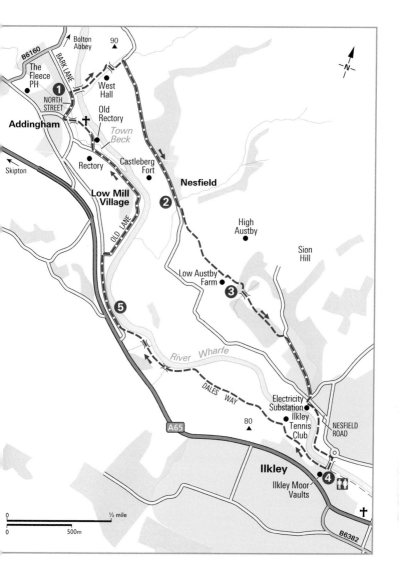

1. Walk 50yds (46m) up the road, and take stone steps down to the right, (signed 'Dales Way'). Turn immediately right again, dropping to cross the River Wharfe on a suspension bridge. Follow a metalled path along a field edge. Turn over a stream at the end and follow a farm track left to emerge on the bend of a minor road. Go right here; after about half a mile (800m) of road walking you reach the little community of Nesfield.

2. About 100yds (91m) beyond the last house and, immediately after the road crosses a stream, bear left up a stony track (signed as a footpath to High Austby). Immediately take a stile between two gates. Cross to the gate in the far-right corner. Through it there is no obvious path, but follow the boundary

on your right, heading in the direction of Low Austby Farm. Carry on in the final field past the farm, bearing slightly left beneath a gnarled oak towards the wood ahead.

3. Cross a footbridge over a stream; beyond a stile you enter woodland. Follow a path downhill, leaving the wood by another step stile. Bear right across the slope of a field to a stile at the far end, to enter more woodland. Follow an obvious path through the trees, before reaching a road via a wall stile. Go right, downhill, until you reach a road junction. Go right again, cross Nesfield Road, and take a path to the left of an electricity substation. Leading to the river, it accompanies the wooded bank to Ilkley's old stone bridge. Cross to the south side.

4. To explore the town, go left by the river through the park. Swing right towards its far end to come out by the ancient church. Otherwise, follow the Dales Way back to Addingham by turning right on a riverside path. At its end, keep ahead along the drive to Ilkley Tennis Club. Reaching the clubhouse, bear off left through a kissing gate across pasture. Partway along the second field, take a kissing gate on the left and walk beside two more fields back to the river. Over a stream, continue through trees. Beyond a second stream, a stony path drops back down to the Wharfe. Carry on at the edge of grazing, emerging at the far end onto a now-quiet lane, once the main Skipton road.

5. Walk right for just over a quarter of a mile (400m) before turning off along Old Lane. Reaching Low Mill village, bear right to follow the street between cottages. At the end, keep ahead on a path that quickly reverts to a lane. After another 0.25 miles (400m), beyond the old Rectory set back within spacious grounds, look for a gate on the right from which steps drop to a tiny arched bridge over Town Beck. Swing left across a pasture in front of the church to join a drive at the far side. Go left but immediately bear off right through a gate over another bridge. Wind between cottages to emerge onto North Road and turn right back to the parking spot.

Where to eat and drink
In Addingham, try The Fleece for traditional pub food. Ilkley has a huge range of places to eat and drink. At the bottom end of Ilkley you are close to the 'The Taps' or the Ilkley Moor Vaults pub as it is officially called, and the Riverside Hotel, which is particularly child-friendly.

While you're there
Addingham lies at the northwestern edge of the county. Just a mile (1.6km) to the north you enter the Yorkshire Dales National Park. By following the B6160 you soon come to Bolton Abbey, with its priory ruins in an idyllic setting by a bend in the River Wharfe.

AROUND LOTHERSDALE ON THE PENNINE WAY

DISTANCE/TIME	4 miles (6.4km) / 2hrs
ASCENT/GRADIENT	816ft (249m) / ▲▲
PATHS	Tracks and field paths, some steep sections, 8 stiles
LANDSCAPE	Pennine moorland, farmland and industrial relics
SUGGESTED MAP	OS Explorer OL21 South Pennines
START/FINISH	Grid reference: SD939472
DOG FRIENDLINESS	Off leads on final section of walk only, from Point 5 onwards
PARKING	Roadside parking on West Road, near junction with Clogger Lane
PUBLIC TOILETS	None on route

Set deep in the rolling countryside to the west of Keighley, Lothersdale is a village of gritstone houses and mill buildings – typical of the small settlements that grew up in the late 18th and early 19th centuries along the river valleys of the West Riding of Yorkshire. The mill dam that you will cross as you enter the village is characteristic of the scale of the industrial enterprise then. Farming and industry had always co-existed here, and today Lothersdale relies on agriculture and tourism – it is a popular stop on the Pennine Way – as well as its role as a base for those who work in the West Yorkshire conurbation.

In the quarry

The Lothersdale district is of particular interest to geologists. As part of the Ribblesdale Fold Belt, there is a notable anticline at Lothersdale, where the limestone has been tilted by the forces of the earth so that it dips significantly – at angles of anything from 20 to 90 degrees from the horizontal. This dramatic effect is best studied at Raygill Quarry, to the west of the village, where the crest of the anticline is exposed in the rock faces. Between 1876 and 1895 over 35,000 tons of barytes was mined at Raygill. This valuable mineral is a sulphate of barium, which is used in drilling processes, as well as in industrial coatings and linings. The quarrying of the fine carboniferous limestone here continued well into the 20th century, but has now ceased, and the flooded quarry workings are now a successful trout fishery.

Raygill was also the site of a discovery, in 1880, of the bones and teeth of several mammals that died in fissures in the rocks in the period between the ice ages. They included remains of mammoth, rhinoceros, lions, bears, bison and hyenas. The bones were taken to Leeds City Museum, where they were damaged by bombing during World War II.

Friends and scholars

The Society of Friends has had a long association with Lothersdale. This once-remote valley provided a haven for Quakers during the persecutions of the 17th century. They built a meeting house here in 1723. It had a gallery with unusually designed hatches that could close to create a separate room. In 1800 the Lothersdale Quakers opened one of the earliest Sunday schools anywhere in the world. The meeting house closed in 1959.

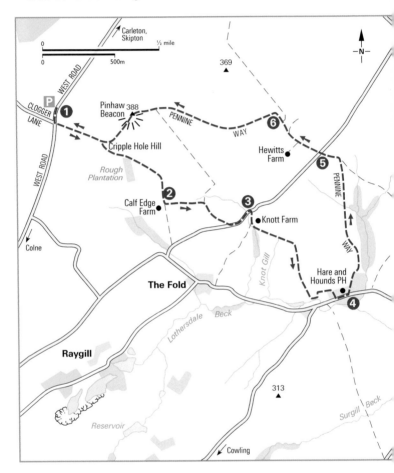

1. From the car park walk downhill towards the mast on the next hilltop. Just before the cattle grid, turn left up a signed track. At the next signpost turn right, off the track. Follow the wall, then bear left to cut off the corner as it bends left. Soon after, cross a stile in the wall on your right. Cross three more stiles then bear left, above a small plantation, then go diagonally right. Go over a stile and continue downhill with a wall on your right, which bends left to reach a signed stile onto a metalled drive.

2. Turn left along the drive. After the cattle grid, bear right along a concrete road and over another cattle grid. Emerge onto a metalled lane and turn left. Follow the lane as it dips to cross a small stream, then immediately turn right.

3. Follow the track, which bends left below a house, then continues across a field with a wall on your left. From the next gate bear right to another gate and

continue down, following the wall on the left towards a pool in the valley. Cross a stile in the corner, turn left immediately through a gate and in a few paces go left and up to join a track. Turn right and follow it to the road. Turn left. Just beyond the Hare and Hounds pub, turn left at the Pennine Way sign.

4. Follow the track uphill to a Pennine Way sign. Turn left here to follow the fence and then the wall on your left, crossing a small stream. Continue straight ahead to a stile beside a gate on your left, signed with an acorn. Go straight across the field to a stone stile onto a lane.

5. Cross the lane and continue up the track ahead, signed 'Pennine Way'. Where the concrete farm track bends left, go straight ahead over a stone stile onto a walled track. Where the walls open out, follow the wall on your left to a stile, then continue to follow the wall on your left until the point at which it bends sharply left.

6. Follow the wall left, go over two plank bridges and continue along the well-worn path, past occasional cairns to the trig point on the hilltop. Follow either of the two downhill paths, which soon rejoin, and continue past the signpost you passed near the start of the walk. Continue downhill to the road and turn right to return to the car parking place.

Where to eat and drink

The Hare and Hounds in Lothersdale is on the route. It has beamed ceilings and real ale, and serves meals at lunchtime and in the evening. Its pleasant beer garden is ideal for children.

What to see

Like many places in the area, Lothersdale has close connections with the Brontës – Haworth is less than 8 miles (12.9km) away. At a house called Stone Gappe (private) on the hillside 0.5 miles (800m) east of Lothersdale, Charlotte Brontë was employed as a governess by the Sidgwick family. She had just left her old school, Roe Head, where she had taught for nearly three years. She was not happy in her employment at Stone Gappe, and left after less than three months there. Like many of Charlotte's early experiences, her time at Stone Gappe was used in her writing; the house appears in the first four chapters of *Jane Eyre* as Gateshead Hall, the scene of Jane's imprisonment in the Red Room and from where she is taken to Lowood School.

While you're there

The far-reaching views from Pinhaw Beacon near the end of the walk are matched in splendour by those from the top of Lund's Tower near Cowling, 3 miles (4.8km) southeast of Lothersdale. Built to either commemorate the Diamond Jubilee of 1897, or the coming of age of Miss Ethel Lund of Malsis Hall down in the valley (or quite possibly both), it shares its ridge with an obelisk, Wainman's Pinnacle, while 0.5 miles (800m) to the south is the 1,000-ton Hitching Stone, said (though who can tell?) to be Yorkshire's largest boulder.

34 ILKLEY MOOR AND THE TWELVE APOSTLES

DISTANCE/TIME	4.5 miles (7.2km) / 2hrs
ASCENT/GRADIENT	875ft (266m) / ▲ ▲
PATHS	Good moorland paths, some steep paths towards end of walk
LANDSCAPE	Mostly open heather moorland and gritstone crags
SUGGESTED MAP	OS Explorer 297 Lower Wharfedale & Washburn Valley
START/FINISH	Grid reference: SE132467
DOG FRIENDLINESS	Under close control at all times
PARKING	Car park below Cow and Calf rocks
PUBLIC TOILETS	At White Wells Spa Cottage and Café

Ilkley Moor is a long ridge of millstone grit, immediately to the south of Ilkley. It's a special place – not just for walkers but for lovers of archaeological relics, too. These extensive heather moors are identified on maps as Rombalds Moor but, thanks to the famous song – Yorkshire's unofficial anthem – Ilkley Moor is how it will always be known.

An ancient ring and a historical spa

The Twelve Apostles is a ring of Bronze Age standing stones sited close to the meeting of two ancient routes across the moor. The 12 slabs of millstone grit (there were probably 20 stones originally, with one at the centre) are arranged in a circle approximately 50ft (15m) in diameter. The tallest stone is little more than 3ft (1m). The circle is the most visible evidence of 7,000 years of occupation of these moors. There are other, smaller circles too, and Ilkley Moor is celebrated for its Bronze Age rock carvings, the most famous of which features a sinuous swastika: traditionally a symbol of good luck, until the Nazis corrupted it. In addition to Pancake and Haystack rocks, seen on this walk, there are dozens of other natural gritstone rock formations. The biggest and best known are the Cow and Calf, close to the start of this walk, where climbers practise their holds and rope work.

Ilkley was a little village until the discovery of mineral springs turned it into a prosperous spa town. Dr William Mcleod arrived here in 1847, and recognised – or perhaps just imagined – the curative properties of cold water. He vigorously promoted what he called the 'Ilkley Cure', a strict regime of exercise and cold baths. Luxurious hotels, known as 'hydros', sprang up around the town to cater for the influx of visitors.

Predating the town's popularity as a spa is White Wells, built in 1700 around one of the original springs. A century later a pair of plunge baths were added, where visitors could enjoy bathing in cold water. Enjoying extensive views over the town, the building is still white.

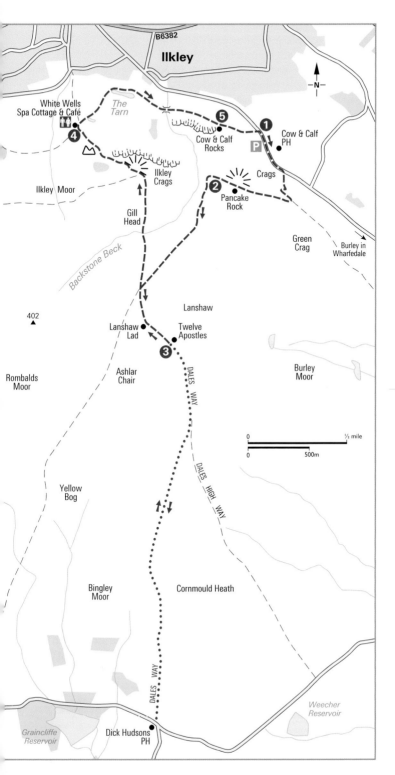

Ilkley

B6382

White Wells
Spa Cottage & Café

The Tarn

④

Ilkley Moor

Ilkley Crags

Gill Head

Backstone Beck

402 ▲

Lanshaw Lad

③

Ashlar Chair

Rombalds Moor

Yellow Bog

Bingley Moor

Graincliffe Reservoir

Cow & Calf Rocks

⑤

P

① Cow & Calf PH

② Crags

Pancake Rock

Green Crag

Burley in Wharfedale

Lanshaw

Twelve Apostles

DALES WAY

Burley Moor

0   ½ mile
0   500m

DALES HIGH WAY

Cornmould Heath

DALES WAY

Weecher Reservoir

Dick Hudsons PH

1. Walk up beside the road, forking right 150yds (137m) beyond the Cow and Calf pub onto a signed footpath. Higher up, swing right and then turn left. At a waymarker, double back right onto the edge and follow it past Pancake Rock. Dip across a path rising along a shallow gully and continue beyond Haystack Rock, joining another path from the left. Keep to the left at several successive forks, swinging parallel to the broad fold containing Backstone Beck, over to the right.

2. After gently rising for 0.75 miles (1.2km) across open moor, the path eventually meets the Bradford–Ilkley Dales Way link. Go left along the paved path, cresting the rise by Lanshaw Lad, a prominent boundary stone to reach the Twelve Apostles, lying just beyond.

3. Retrace your steps from the Twelve Apostles, this time staying with the paved Dales Way. Keep ahead beyond the end of the flags, crossing a small stream and then Backstone Beck at Gill Head. Climbing away, take the left fork past a waymarker. After 0.25 miles (400m), keep ahead at a crossing. The path then swings left in a steep descent, eventually leading to White Wells.

4. Swing right in front of the café and bathhouse, the path passing a small pond and slanting down the rocky hillside to meet a metalled path. Go right, taking either branch around the tarn. Leave up steps at the far end, the ongoing path later dipping to cross Backstone Beck. Over the bridge, bear left and stick with the main trail. Approaching the Cow and Calf Rocks, ignore a crossing path and keep ahead to skirt below the outcrop.

5. It's worth taking a few minutes to investigate the rocks and watch climbers practising their belays and traverses. From here, a paved path leads back to the car park.

Extending the walk A classic extension of this walk takes you across the moor from the Twelve Apostles (Point 3) to The Dick Hudsons pub, returning by the same route.

Where to eat and drink
The Cow and Calf, at the start of the walk, serves seasonal food and cask ales. If you take the extension to the walk, The Dick Hudsons, named after a 19th-century landlord, offers wholesome food and wholesome views.

What to see
Many rocks on Ilkley Moor are decorated with 'cup and ring' patterns – including the Pancake Rock, near the start of this walk. Many more rock carvings can be found if you take the time to search for them.

While you're there
Ilkley Moor is an intriguingly ancient landscape, criss-crossed by old tracks. This walk and its extension offer short and long options, but you could explore for weeks without walking the same path twice. An east-west walk from the Cow and Calf will take you along the moorland ridge, with terrific views of Ilkley and Wharfedale for most of the way.

BURLEY IN WHARFEDALE

35

DISTANCE/TIME	5 miles (8km) / 2hrs 15min
ASCENT/GRADIENT	966ft (294m) / ▲ ▲
PATHS	Good tracks and moorland paths, several stiles
LANDSCAPE	Moor and arable farmland
SUGGESTED MAP	OS Explorer 297 Lower Wharfedale & Washburn Valley
START/FINISH	Grid reference: SE163458
DOG FRIENDLINESS	Can be off leads but watch for grazing sheep
PARKING	Roadside parking near station
PUBLIC TOILETS	None on route

According to the legend, a giant called Rombald used to live in these parts. While striding across the moor that now bears his name (in some versions of the story he was being chased by his angry wife) he dislodged a stone from a gritstone outcrop, and thus created the Calf, of the Cow and Calf Rocks (see walk 34). Giants such as Rombald and Wade – and even the Devil himself – were apparently busy all over Yorkshire, dropping stones or creating big holes in the ground. It was perhaps an appealing way to explain the more unusual features of the landscape. Rombalds Moor is pitted with old quarries, from which good quality stone was won.

The Hermit of Rombalds Moor

At Burley Woodhead a public house called The Hermit commemorates Job Senior, a local character with a chequered career. Job worked as a farm labourer, before succumbing to the demon drink. He met an elderly widow of independent means, who lived in a cottage at Coldstone Beck, on the edge of Rombalds Moor. Thinking he might get his hands on her money and home, Job married her. Though she died soon after, Job took no profit. The family of her first husband pulled the cottage down, in Job's absence, leaving him homeless and penniless once more. Enraged, he built himself a tiny hovel from the ruins of the house. Here he lived in filth and squalor on a diet of home-grown potatoes, which he roasted on a peat fire. He must have cut a strange figure, with a coat of multicoloured patches and trousers held up with twine. He had long, lank hair, a matted beard and his legs were bandaged with straw. He made slow, rheumatic progress around Rombalds Moor with the aid of two crooked sticks. His eccentric lifestyle soon had people flocking to see him. He offered weather predictions, and even advised visitors about their love lives. The possessor of a remarkable voice, he 'sang for his supper' as he lay on his bed of dried bracken and heather. These impromptu performances encouraged Job to sing in nearby villages, and even in the theatres of Leeds and Bradford. His speciality was sacred songs, which he would deliver with great feeling. Nevertheless, accommodation was never forthcoming, forcing him to bed

124

down in barns or outhouses. It was while staying in a barn that he was struck down with cholera. He was taken to Carlton Workhouse, where he died in 1857, aged 77. He is buried in the churchyard of Burley in Wharfedale. His life is commemorated in the old sign hanging over the entrance to The Hermit Inn.

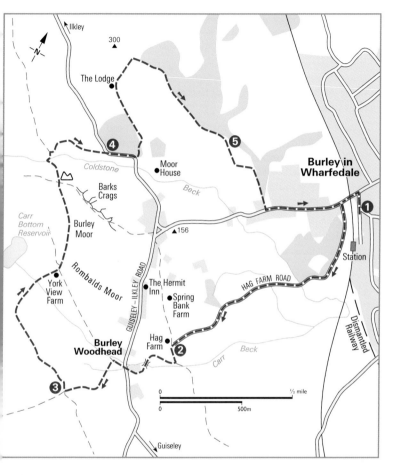

1. From the station, walk back to Station Road, turn left to cross underneath the line and go left along a quiet lane. Follow the lane past houses and between fields up to Hag Farm.

2. When the track wheels right, into the farmyard, keep left on a track to a stile and a gate. Follow a wall downhill for 100yds (91m) to a gap stile in the wall. Don't pass through, but turn right, climbing beside a stream up to a stile. Carry on uphill, crossing two more stiles and then a footbridge across the stream. Continue up to cottages, winding out between them to meet the Guiseley–Ilkley road. (To visit The Hermit Inn, go right here for 0.25 miles/400m.) Cross the road and continue on a stony track opposite. After 50yds (46m), leave left to ford a stream. Follow a path uphill through trees and then between walls to a gate. Turn right beside the wall, which soon curves away, leaving you heading upwards on a trod (rough footpath).

3. Meet a stony track and follow it to the right, along the moorland edge. Follow a wall to a stile by a gate. Immediately after, keep right when the track forks. Keep to the right again as you approach a small brick building. Route-finding is now easy, as the track wheels around a farm. At the next farm (called York View because on a clear day, you can see York Minster from here) branch left off the main track, gradually descending by a wall on your right. As you approach a third farm, look out for two barns and a gate, on the right. They stand opposite an indistinct path to the left, which curves around a small quarry. Now enjoy some level walking through bracken with great views over Lower Wharfedale. After 0.25 miles (400m), drop into a narrow ravine to cross Coldstone Beck. As you climb away, bear right and follow a path downhill to meet a road by a sharp bend.

4. Walk 100yds (91m) down the road to another sharp bend. Turn off along Stead Lane, a stony track which leads past several houses, to continue between the fields beyond. After passing a wooden chalet, leave the track as it swings left towards a farm, dropping through a kissing gate to the right. Walk away beside the wood on your left. Beyond another kissing gate, keep by the right-hand boundary, leaving at the far side to follow a fenced path ahead.

5. Reaching a track, go right, but after 200yds (183m), bear off left along a path which leads to a second track within trees. Follow it right to the road and turn left back to the station.

Where to eat and drink

The Hermit Inn is a welcoming stone-built pub in Burley Woodhead. During the walk it is easy to make a short detour to the inn, with its views of Wharfedale. Alternatively, the village of Burley boasts a number of places to get a bite to eat.

What to see

Rombalds Moor is home to red grouse, often claimed to be the only truly indigenous British bird. Grouse take off from their heather hiding places with heart-stopping suddenness, with their unmistakable and evocative cry of 'go back, go back, go back'. The moorland habitat is carefully managed to maintain a supply of young heather for the grouse to nest and feed in as grouse shooting is a lucrative business. The season begins on the 'Glorious Twelfth' of August.

While you're there

Ilkley's parish church, which can trace its origins to the 7th century, contains three beautiful Anglo-Saxon crosses. It occupies the site of a Roman fort overlooking the River Wharfe and, although only a short stretch of wall remains visible, many of the artefacts discovered during excavations can be seen in the nearby Ilkley Manor House. Other exhibits describe the prehistoric art scattered across the surrounding hillsides and explore Ilkley's growth as a spa town.

36

HAREWOOD AND AROUND THE HAREWOOD ESTATE

DISTANCE/TIME	7 miles (11.3km) / 2hrs 45min
ASCENT/GRADIENT	693ft (211m) / ▲
PATHS	Good paths and parkland tracks all the way
LANDSCAPE	Arable farmland and parkland
SUGGESTED MAP	OS Explorer 289 Leeds
START/FINISH	Grid reference: SE334450
DOG FRIENDLINESS	Keep on leads in conservation areas, near sheep and deer and on roads
PARKING	From the traffic lights at junction of A61 and A659 (Harewood Ave), take A659 and park in first lay-by on left, some way down the road
PUBLIC TOILETS	None on route

The grand old houses of West Yorkshire tend to be in the form of 'Halifax' houses (such as East Riddlesden Hall). Self-made yeomen and merchant clothiers built their mansions to show the world that they'd made their 'brass'. But Harewood House, on the edge of Leeds, is more ambitious, and is still one of the great treasure houses of England.

Vision into reality

The Harewood Estate passed through a number of wealthy hands during the 16th and 17th centuries, eventually being bought by the Lascelles family who still own the house. Edwin Lascelles left the 12th-century castle in its ruinous state, to overlook the broad valley of the River Wharfe, but demolished the old hall. He wanted to create something special in its place and hired the best architects and designers to turn his vision into grand reality. John Carr of York created a veritable palace, in an imposing neoclassical style, and laid out the estate village of Harewood too. The foundations were laid in 1759; 12 years later the house was finished. Thomas Chippendale, born in nearby Otley, made furniture for every room, as part of the house's original plans. Inside are paintings by J M W Turner and Thomas Girtin, who both stayed and painted there. Turner was particularly taken with the area, producing pictures of many local landmarks. The sumptuous interior, however, is in sharp contrast to the world of those below stairs, whose life and work is depicted in the Old Kitchen and servants' quarters.

The extensive grounds were preened and groomed to be as magnificent as the house. They were shaped by Lancelot 'Capability' Brown, the most renowned designer of the English landscape. In addition to the formal gardens, he created the lake and the woodland paths you visit on this walk. Like many stately homes, Harewood House has had to earn its keep in recent years. The bird garden was the first commercial venture, but now the house hosts a range of events such as art exhibitions, vintage car rallies and open-air concerts.

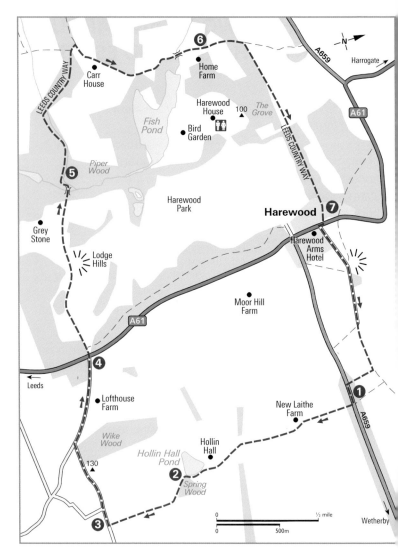

1. From the lay-by walk 50yds (46m) away from the village of Harewood, cross the road and walk right down the access track to New Laithe Farm. Pass left of the farm buildings to pick up a gravel track heading into the valley bottom. Go through a gate and bear half left up a field, towards Hollin Hall. Keep left of the buildings to pass Hollin Hall Pond.

2. Beyond the pond, swing left around the corner of Spring Wood and follow a track at the field-edge to the top corner. Through gates continue up the hill, the track later becoming enclosed and ending at a junction.

3. Go right along the crest of the hill to have easy, level walking on an enclosed sandy track (now following the Leeds Country Way). Keep straight ahead past

a junction, through a gate. Skirt woodland to emerge onto a lane. Follow it right to reach the A61.

4. Cross the road to enter the Harewood Estate (via the righthand gate, between imposing gateposts). Follow the broad track ahead, through landscaped parkland, soon getting views of Harewood House to the right. Enter woodland through a gate, turning immediately left after a stone bridge.

5. After 100yds (91m), bear right at a fork and keep with the main track. It later swings right, dipping across a stream and eventually reaching a crossing. Go right down to another junction and turn right again, the way curving left out of the trees to pass Carr House. Carry on at the edge of the park, then swing left again at the next junction, rising beside a high wall to meet a metalled drive. Bear left to a crossroads and keep ahead over a bridge and another crossing, climbing beside the Home Farm complex.

6. Follow the drive into the deer park, keeping right at the next junction. Continue through woodland until you come to the few houses that comprise the estate village of Harewood.

7. Cross the main A61 road and walk right, for 50yds (46m), to take a metalled drive just before the Harewood Arms Hotel. Beyond Maltkiln House, the way continues as a gated field track, with views over Lower Wharfedale. Carry on through a second gate for a further 350yds (320m) to a junction and go right over a cattle grid along a permissive bridleway, before regaining the A659 beside the lay-by.

Where to eat and drink

Apart from designing the house itself, John Carr was also responsible for the estate village of Harewood. The neat terraced houses have architectural echoes of the big house. Almost opposite the main gates of Harewood House is the Harewood Arms Hotel, a former coaching inn that offers the chance of a drink or meal towards the end of the walk and a beer garden in good weather.

What to see

The red kite, a beautiful fork-tailed bird of prey, is once again becoming a familiar sight. Centuries of persecution had brought the species close to extinction in England, but Harewood has successfully reintroduced them to this part of Yorkshire. Now, during winter and spring, up to 80 birds can gather as evening falls. Look out too for other hunting birds, including three of Britain's owl species.

While you're there

As well as the house with its fabulous state rooms and art treasures, there are endless paths among the terraces and gardens. There is much to see in the bird garden, which houses exotic and rare species from around the world. Complete the walk in the morning to work up a healthy appetite for lunch and spend the rest of the day exploring the house and grounds.

WETHERBY AND THE RIVER WHARFE

DISTANCE/TIME	4 miles (6.4km) / 1hr 30min
ASCENT/GRADIENT	252ft (77m) / ▲
PATHS	Field paths and good tracks, a little road-walking
LANDSCAPE	Arable land, mostly on the flat
SUGGESTED MAP	OS Explorer 289 Leeds
START/FINISH	Grid reference: SE404480
DOG FRIENDLINESS	Keep on leads along roads and by racecourse
PARKING	Free car parking in Wilderness car park, on right immediately over bridge when approaching Wetherby from the south
PUBLIC TOILETS	Wetherby

Wetherby, at the northeast corner of the county, is not your typical West Yorkshire town. Most of the houses are built of pale stone, topped with red-tiled roofs – a type of architecture more usually found in North Yorkshire. With its riverside developments and air of prosperity, the Wetherby of today is a favoured place to live. The flat, arable landscape, too, is very different from Pennine Yorkshire. Here, on the fringes of the Vale of York, the soil is rich and dark and productive – the fields divided up by fences and hedgerows rather than dry-stone walls.

Historic town

The town has a long history. A brief glance at an Ordnance Survey map reveals that Wetherby grew up around a tight curve in the River Wharfe. Its importance as a river crossing was recognised by the building of a castle, possibly in the 12th century, of which only the foundations remain. The first mention of a bridge was in 1233. A few years later, in 1240, the Knights Templar were granted a royal charter to hold a market in Wetherby. At Flint Mill, passed on this walk, flints were ground for use in the pottery industry of Leeds. The town also had two corn mills, powered by water from the River Wharfe. The distinctive, restored weir helped to maintain a good head of water to turn the waterwheels.

In general though, the Industrial Revolution made little impression on Wetherby. The town grew in importance not from what it made, but from where it was situated. In the days of coach travel, the 400-mile (643km) trip between London and Edinburgh was quite an ordeal for passengers and horses alike. And Wetherby, at the halfway point of the journey, became a convenient stop for mail and passenger coaches. The trade was busiest during the second half of the 18th century, when the town had upwards of 40 inns and alehouses. Coaching inns catered for weary travellers and provided stabling for the horses. The Angel, known as 'the Halfway House', had stables for more than 100 horses. The Great North Road ran across the town's splendid arched bridge, and right through the middle of the town. When the railway arrived in the 1840s, Wetherby's role as a staging post went into decline. The Great North Road was eventually rerouted around the town, and became known simply as the A1 and now the A1(M). In 1964, Wetherby lost its railway too. Ironically, a town that had once been synonymous with coach travel is now a peaceful place, reinventing itself once again as an upmarket commuter town.

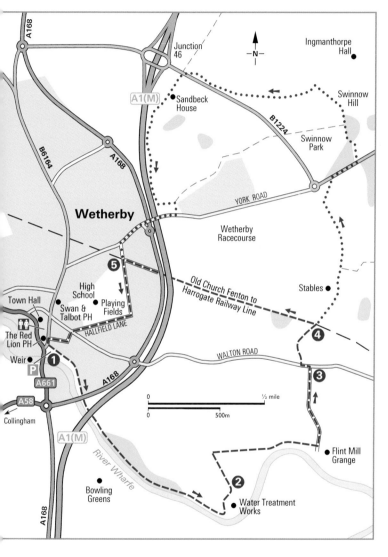

1. Walk to the far end of the car park, to follow a path at the foot of low cliffs beside the River Wharfe. You pass in quick succession beneath the shallow spans of three modern bridges, carrying the A168 and A1(M) roads across the Wharfe. Emerging beyond, walk the length of a narrow pasture, passing through a kissing gate at the far end by Wetherby's Water Treatment Works.

2. Turn left beside the perimeter fence to the plant entrance and go left again along a metalled drive. After 300yds (274m), meeting a junction of tracks at the top of a rise, turn off right along a field track. Carry on along the top of a wooded bank that falls to the River Wharfe, emerging onto the bend of another drive at Flint Mill Grange. Go left and walk out to the main road.

3. Turn left along Walton Road. After 75yds (69m) cross to a gated drive on the right, an entrance to Wetherby Racecourse and a bridleway through to York Road. Walk for 0.25 miles (400m) to meet a crossing track. The longer walk continues along the drive ahead.

4. To return directly to Wetherby, however, turn left, dropping onto the trackbed of the old Church Fenton-to-Harrogate railway line, which carried its last train in 1964. A mile's (1.6km) easy walking takes you to the A1(M) motorway, raised up on an embankment as it skirts around Wetherby. Take the underpass beneath the road, and keep ahead along Freemans Way, until you meet Hallfield Lane.

5. Walk left, along Hallfield Lane, following it right around the playing fields of Wetherby High School towards the town centre. At the end, bear left into Nags Lane, right along Victoria Street and then go left back to the river.

Extending the walk You can extend the walk to see more of Wetherby's famous racecourse by leaving the main walk at Point 4 and following firstly a waymarked bridleway and then Sandbeck Lane, before crossing the motorway bridge to return to the main walk at Point 5.

Where to eat and drink
As a market town, and a staging post on the Great North Road, Wetherby is well provided with a choice of pubs, cafés and old coaching inns. For example, The Red Lion on the High Street near the start of the walk serves traditional bar meals at very reasonable prices. It's open every day.

What to see
Unlike many towns in West Yorkshire, Wetherby still holds its general market every Thursday, with the stalls arranged around the handsome little town hall. Nearby are the Shambles, a row of colonnaded stalls built in 1811 to house a dozen butchers' shops.

While you're there
Wetherby's nearest neighbour is Boston Spa which, like Ilkley, became a prosperous spa town on the River Wharfe. It was the accidental discovery, in 1744, of a mineral spring that changed the town's fortunes. The salty taste and sulphurous smell were enough to convince people that the spring water had health-giving properties, and a pump room and bathhouse were built to cater for well-heeled visitors. The town's great days as a spa town are over but, with some splendid Georgian buildings, it has retained an air of elegance.

GOLDEN ACRE PARK AND BREARY MARSH

DISTANCE/TIME	6 miles (9.7km) / 2hrs 15min
ASCENT/GRADIENT	392ft (119m) / ▲
PATHS	Good paths, tracks and quiet roads, many stiles
LANDSCAPE	Parkland, woods and arable country
SUGGESTED MAP	OS Explorer 297 Lower Wharfedale & Washburn Valley
START/FINISH	Grid reference: SE266417
DOG FRIENDLINESS	Keep on leads at all times
PARKING	Golden Acre Park car park, across road from park itself, on A660 just south of Bramhope
PUBLIC TOILETS	Golden Acre Park, at start of walk

Leeds is fortunate to have so many green spaces. Some, like Roundhay Park, are long established; others, like Kirkstall Valley Nature Reserve, have been created from post-industrial wasteland. But none have had a more chequered history than Golden Acre Park, which is 6 miles (9.7km) north of the city on the main A660.

Amusement park

The park originally opened in 1932 as an amusement park. The attractions included a miniature railway, nearly 2 miles (3.2km) in length, complete with dining car. The lake was the centre of much activity, with motor launches, dinghies for hire and races by the Yorkshire Hydroplane Racing Squadron. An open-air lido known, somewhat exotically, as the Blue Lagoon, offered unheated swimming. The Winter Gardens Dance Hall boasted that it had 'the largest dance floor in Yorkshire'. Though visitors initially flocked to Golden Acre Park, the novelty soon wore off. By the end of the 1938 season, the amusement park had closed down and was sold to Leeds City Council. The site was subsequently transformed into botanical gardens – a process that's continued ever since. The hillside overlooking the lake has been lovingly planted with trees and unusual plants, including rock gardens and fine displays of rhododendrons. The boats are long gone; the lake is now a haven for wildfowl. Within these 127 acres (51ha) – the 'Golden Acre' name was as fanciful as 'the Blue Lagoon' – is a wide variety of wildlife habitats, from open heathland to an old quarry. Lovers of birds, trees and flowers will find plenty to interest them at every season of the year.

One of the few echoes of the original Golden Acre Park is a café situated close to the entrance. Reflecting the park's increasing popularity with local people, a large car park has been built on the opposite side of the main road, with pedestrian access to the park via a tunnel beneath the road. This intriguing park offers excellent walking, and wheelchair users, too, can make a circuit of the lake on a broad path.

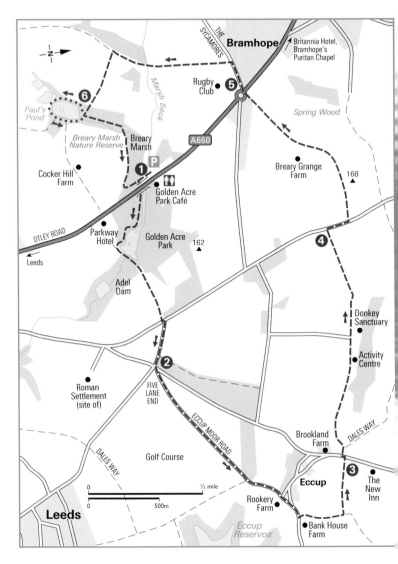

1. From the southern corner of the car park, an underpass leads into Golden Acre Park. Turn right on a path that winds to the far end of the lake. Ignore the path heading off left across the lake dam and walk forward out of the park onto a tree-lined bridlepath. Go left beside the park boundary to emerge at a junction of lanes. Take the one that's ahead, up to the aptly named Five Lane End junction.

2. Take the second road on the left (Eccup Moor Road). Stick with it for a mile (1.6km) past junctions until you reach the outbuildings of Bank House Farm, where a waymarked bridleway leaves on the left. It soon narrows to a hedged path. About 50yds (46m) before the footpath later swings right, take a stile in the fence on your left. Follow the field-edge away to a wall stile and continue

forward across another field to emerge onto a lane (The New Inn is then just along to your right).

3. Go left along the road for just 20yds (18m) to take a stile on your right. Keep ahead over an intersection to join another track, which leads forward to a gate and stile. Carry on for 150yds (137m) by the boundary to a waypost and bear right across the pasture to a stile in the end wall. Walk on towards an activity centre, bypassing it through a couple of kissing gates to meet a track. Go right and immediately left along an enclosed grass track past a donkey sanctuary. When it finishes, maintain your direction walking beside successive fields to reach a road.

4. Go right for 150yds (137m) then take a waymarked kissing gate on the left. Follow the field-edge path by the left fence. Beyond two more kissing gates bear left across another field behind Breary Grange Farm to a ladder stile beyond a large oak. Maintain the same direction to a stile at the far corner and continue across a final field. Leave over a stile next to buildings onto the A660 by a roundabout.

5. Cross the main road and turn into The Sycamores. Walk past the Rugby Club, but some 100yds (91m) further on, leave through a kissing gate on the left. Head away at the edge of successive fields towards a wood. Crossing a beck, carry on beside the trees. Reaching a stile, swing left along a track towards a farmhouse. Continue on the field path beyond to a gate that leads into the Breary Marsh Nature Reserve.

6. The path heading off sharp right makes a circuit around the lake, a pleasant extension if you're not pushed for time. Otherwise, bear slightly right onto a path below the foot of the dam. At a junction, go left with the Leeds Country Way, signed towards the A660. Wind with the bridleway across a bridge but, at the next junction, turn left back to the car park.

Where to eat and drink

It requires the shortest of detours, at about the halfway point of this walk, to visit The New Inn, near Eccup. A sign welcomes walkers – as do the open fires and beer garden – and an extensive menu will whet your appetite. The Golden Acre Park Café, in the park of the same name, offers everything from a snack to a full meal.

What to see

Look for the damp-loving alder trees in Breary Marsh. Their seeds float on the water. During winter you should see little siskins (a type of finch) feeding on the seeds, of which they are particularly fond. You may also spy the vivid caterpillar of the alder moth.

While you're there

Bramhope's Puritan Chapel, adjacent to the entrance to the Britannia Hotel on the A660, is a small, simple chapel built in 1649, by devout Puritan Robert Dyneley. Although it's generally locked, peering through the windows reveals its original furnishings, including box-pews and a three-deck pulpit.

RURAL LEEDS AND THE MEANWOOD VALLEY

DISTANCE/TIME	5.25 miles (8.4km) / 2hrs 15min
ASCENT/GRADIENT	729ft (222m) / ▲
PATHS	Urban paths, parkland and woodland paths
LANDSCAPE	Mostly woodland
SUGGESTED MAP	OS Explorer 289 Leeds
START	Grid reference: SE293350
FINISH	Grid reference: SE270402
DOG FRIENDLINESS	Keep on leads near roads
PARKING	Street parking off main road at both ends of the walk; bus services 1 and X84 operate between the two points
PUBLIC TOILETS	In Meanwood Park

This, the only linear walk in this book, is a splendid ramble, surprisingly rural in aspect throughout, even though it begins just a stone's throw from the bustling heart of Leeds. You start among the terraces of redbrick houses that are so typical of the city, and five minutes later you are in delightful woodland.

Linking with the Dales Way

The walk follows the first 5 miles (8km) of the Dales Way link path from Leeds to Ilkley (the walk's official starting point). This link path begins at Woodhouse Moor Park – where fairs and circuses have long pitched their tents.

The path follows Woodhouse Ridge into Meanwood Park and along the Meanwood Valley, cocooned against creeping suburbia by a slim sliver of woodland. The route is also promoted as the Meanwood Valley Trail, so there are regular waymarkers to keep you on track.

Parklife

Leeds is fortunate to have so many parks within the city limits, from long established green spaces such as Roundhay Park to newer parks created from brownfield sites, once the site of industry. The first few miles of this walk are through some of this pleasant parkland. Then, after crossing beneath the busy Leeds ring road, you will have the more natural surroundings of Adel Woods to enjoy.

The walk finishes near Adel church, dedicated to St John the Baptist. Though small, it is one of the most perfectly proportioned Norman churches in the country, having been built about 1170. The ornamental stone carving is noteworthy – especially the four arches framing the doorway. From Adel, there's a reliable bus service back to Woodhouse Moor – but check the timetable before you set out.

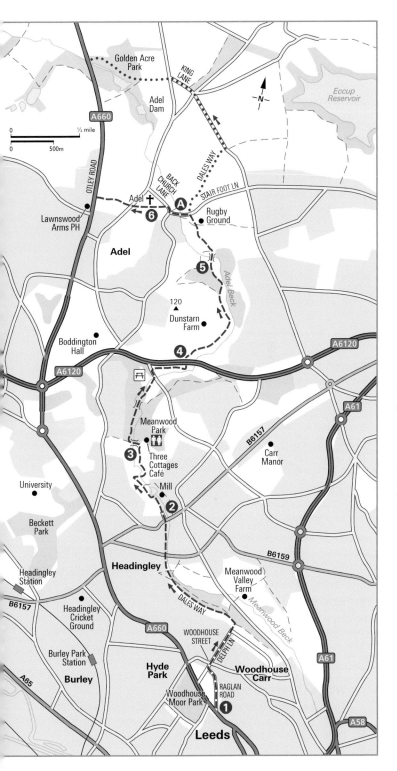

Golden Acre Park

KING LANE

Eccup Reservoir

Adel Dam

A660

N

0   ½ mile
0   500m

OTLEY ROAD

DALES WAY

BACK CHURCH LANE

STAIR FOOT LN

Adel † **6** **A**

Rugby Ground

Lawnswood Arms PH

Adel

5

Adel Beck

120 ▲
Dunstarn Farm

Boddington Hall

A6120

4

A6120

A61

Meanwood Park

B6157

Carr Manor

3

Three Cottages Café

University

Mill

2

Beckett Park

B6159

Meanwood Valley Farm

Headingley Station

Headingley

Meanwood Beck

B6157

Headingley Cricket Ground

DALES WAY

Burley Park Station

A660

WOODHOUSE STREET

DELPH LN

Hyde Park

Woodhouse Carr

A65

Burley

Woodhouse Moor Park

RAGLAN ROAD

1

A61

Leeds

A58

1. Walk down Raglan Road and on along Cathcart Street. At the T-junction, turn right onto Rampart Road, cross Woodhouse Street, and walk ahead up Delph Lane. At the end, go forward through a gap and left onto the higher path along Woodhouse Ridge. Keep with the main trail to a barrier. Where it splits, take the middle option to Grove Lane. There, cross to the path opposite, which shortly emerges at Monk Bridge Road.

2. Cross the road into Highbury Lane, recovering the path beside Meanwood Beck beyond its end. At a junction by a converted mill, go left and then right onto a path between allotments. Keep on to emerge onto a street and walk ahead. After 100yds (91m), by a postbox, turn right into Meanwood Park. Follow the drive to reach a car park. Pass through and swing left onto a lane that leads to a terrace of stone cottages, Hustlers Row.

3. Near the houses drop left along a stony track to cross a footbridge over Meanwood Beck. Bear right just beyond at a fork and head upstream above the beck, shortly rising along a raised bank beside a disued mill leat. Ignoring side paths, it eventually leads to a pair of bridges. Swing over the bridge on the right above a weir and walk forward to a broad path. Go left to emerge from the trees through a gate. Carry on at the edge of a field into more trees, coming out by a picnic site onto a lane. Follow the lane left but, just before reaching a junction with a main road, turn off along an unmarked track on the right. It runs below the embankment before heading through an underpass.

4. Take some steps, at the far end, onto a path that follows Adel Beck. Keep left of the next pile of boulders, rising to a path along the fringe of the woodland. Keep to this higher path until you eventually reach a major fork. Bear right, following an aqueduct across the dip of the valley. Curving left, the path continues through Adel Woods, in time meeting a prominent junction.

5. The Meanwood Valley Trail is signed left, dropping across a stone slab bridge and climbing steps to a small pond. Cross the small feeder stream and fork right. Occasional wayposts mark the ongoing path, which shortly emerges to run at the edge of more open ground. Joining a broader path keep left, finally emerging through a car park onto Stair Foot Lane. Go left, dropping through a dip and up to a junction. Turn right along Back Church Lane but, as that then bears right, keep ahead along a path to Adel church.

6. Walk past the church and leave the churchyard by a collection of coffins and millstones. Cross the road and take a field path opposite. Bear half left across the next field to the Otley Road (A660). Turn left to find a bus stop, opposite the Lawnswood Arms, for the bus back to Woodhouse Moor, in Leeds.

Extending the walk To extend the walk by 1.5 miles (2.4km), don't turn left down Stair Foot Lane (at Point A), but take the track ahead, and turn left when you come to King Lane. This will bring you out at Golden Acre Park, near Bramhope (on the X84 bus route for getting back to Leeds).

Where to eat and drink

There are several pubs just off route during this walk, or wait until the finishing point where you will find the Lawnswood Arms. The Three Cottages Café is also worth a visit at Meanwood Park

SHIPLEY GLEN TRAMWAY AND BAILDON MOOR

DISTANCE/TIME	4 miles (6.4km) / 1hr 45min
ASCENT/GRADIENT	964ft (294m) / ▲ ▲
PATHS	Moor and field paths
LANDSCAPE	Moorland, fields and gritstone rocks
SUGGESTED MAP	OS Explorer 288 Bradford & Huddersfield
START/FINISH	Grid reference: SE131389
DOG FRIENDLINESS	Keep on leads by roads or near livestock
PARKING	Lay-bys on Glen Road, between Bracken Hall Countryside Centre and Old Glen House pub
PUBLIC TOILETS	In Saltaire, near railway station

For the people of Shipley and Saltaire, Baildon Moor has long represented a taste of the countryside on their doorsteps. Mill-hands could leave the mills and cramped terraced streets behind, and breathe clean Pennine air. They could listen to the song of the skylark and the cry of the curlew. There were heather moors to tramp across, gritstone rocks to scramble up and, at Shipley Glen, springy sheep-grazed turf on which to spread out a picnic blanket.

Fun on the moors

There was also once a funfair to visit – in fact, a veritable theme park. Towards the end of the 19th century Shipley Glen was owned by a Colonel Maude, who created a number of attractions, including the Switchback Railway, Marsden's Menagerie, the Horse Tramway and the Aerial Runway. More sedate pleasures could be found at the Camera Obscura, the boating lake in the Japanese garden, and the Temperance Tea Room and Coffee House.

Sam Wilson, a local entrepreneur, created the Shipley Glen Tramway in 1895. Saltaire people could now stroll through Roberts Park, past the steely gazed statue of Sir Titus Salt, and enjoy the tram ride to the top of the glen. Thousands of people would clamber, each weekend, onto the little cable-hauled 'toastrack' cars. The heyday of Shipley Glen was during the Edwardian era when as many as 17,000 people would take the tramway up to the pleasure gardens. Losing out to more sophisticated entertainments, however, Shipley Glen went into a slow decline. Sadly, all the attractions are now gone, but you can still take the ride on the tramway – which runs on Sunday afternoons throughout the year (weather permitting). There is an attractive souvenir shop at the top, while the bottom station houses a small museum and replica Edwardian shop. The Old Glen House is still a popular pub, though the former Temperance Tea Room and Coffee House is now the Bracken Hall Countryside Centre. Local people still enjoy the freedom of the heather moorland. Despite all the changes, Shipley Glen retains a stubbornly old-fashioned air, and is all the better for it.

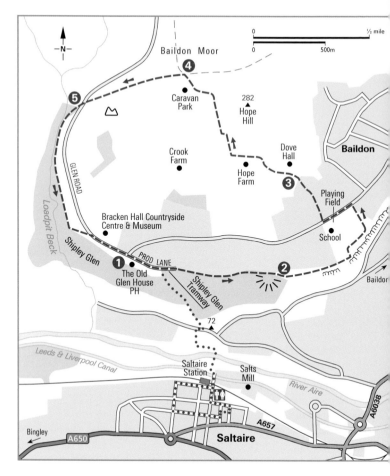

1. Walk down Glen Road, passing The Old Glen House pub. Continue as the road becomes Prod Lane, signed as a cul-de-sac. Where the road ends at the entrance to the Shipley Glen Tramway, keep straight ahead to locate an enclosed path to the right of a house. Follow this path, with houses on your left, and woodland to your right. As you come to a metal barrier, ignore a path to the left. Keep straight on downhill. About 100yds (91m) beyond the barrier, there is a choice of paths; bear left here, contouring the steep hillside and soon getting good views over Saltaire, Shipley and the Aire Valley.

2. Keep going as a path later joins from the right, undulating through scrub and more open heath beneath the old quarried face of a sandstone cliff. After a further 0.25 miles (400m), watch for a stepped path and handrail climbing to the left. At the top, turn right on a fenced path that skirts two sides of a school playing field. Emerging onto a road, cross and go left for 150yds (137m). Drawing level with the entrance to the primary school, turn off onto a narrow, enclosed path that climbs between the houses on the right. Meeting a street higher up, cross to the ongoing path. Continue up to a gate, which opens onto the bottom of a sloping pasture.

3. Go half left uphill to a kissing gate at the far corner of the field. Head out to join an access track along the field top to Hope Farm. Walk past the buildings on a cinder track, leaving just before its end onto a bridleway through a gate on the right. Emerging onto Baildon Moor, the onward path runs alongside the wall on the left. Keep straight on beyond the corner towards a caravan park. Cross a metalled track leading to the campsite and keep ahead to the corner of the boundary wall. Swing left to walk on beside it.

4. Walk gradually downhill towards the distant suburbs of Bingley. When the wall bears left, keep straight ahead, through bracken, more steeply downhill. Cross a metalled track and carry on down to meet Glen Road again.

5. Follow the path along the rocky edge of wooded Shipley Glen, leading you back to the Bracken Hall Countryside Centre and Museum and your car.

Extending the walk The walk can be extended by taking the tramway or adjacent path down into the valley and exploring Salts Mill and the lovely village of Saltaire.

Where to eat and drink
Sir Titus Salt wouldn't allow public houses in Saltaire, but that prohibition didn't extend to Shipley Glen, where The Old Glen House, near the upper tramway station, is open for lunches and evening meals from Tuesday to Saturday and lunch on Sunday. The food is locally sourced wherever possible, with fresh herbs coming from the garden. You'll find local beers on tap too, such as Saltaire Blonde and Timothy Taylor's Landlord.

What to see
Call in at the Bracken Hall Countryside Centre and Museum on Glen Road, which has a number of interesting displays about the history of Shipley Glen, its flora and its fauna. There are also temporary exhibitions on particular themes, interactive features and a programme of children's activities throughout the year. The gift shop sells maps, guides, natural history books and ice creams.

While you're there
Be sure to visit Salts Mill, a giant of a building on a truly epic scale. At the height of production 3,000 people worked here. There were 1,200 looms clattering away, weaving as much as 30,000 yards of cloth every working day. The mill is a little quieter these days – with a permanent exhibition of artworks by David Hockney, another of Bradford's most famous sons.

BINGLEY AND THE ST IVES ESTATE

DISTANCE/TIME	6.25 miles (10.1km) / 2hrs 45min
ASCENT/GRADIENT	1,247ft (380m) / ▲ ▲
PATHS	Good paths and tracks throughout, several stiles
LANDSCAPE	Woodland, park and river
SUGGESTED MAP	OS Explorer 288 Bradford & Huddersfield
START/FINISH	Grid reference: SE107391
DOG FRIENDLINESS	Can be off leads on St Ives Estate
PARKING	Car parks in Bingley
PUBLIC TOILETS	In Myrtle Place by the park

Sitting astride both the River Aire and the Leeds and Liverpool Canal, in a steep-sided valley, Bingley is a typical West Yorkshire town. With its locks, wharves and plethora of mills, the town grew in size and importance during the 19th century as the textile trades expanded. But Bingley's pre-eminence did not begin with the Industrial Revolution; it is, in fact, one of the county's oldest settlements, with its market charter being granted by King John as far back as 1212. Bingley has a number of splendid old buildings, such as the town hall, parish church, butter cross, the old market hall and the Old White Horse, a venerable coaching inn, where King John is reputed to have stayed. However, Bingley has more than its fair share of modern buildings around the town centre.

By the river
The River Aire rises close to the village of Malham, in the limestone dales of North Yorkshire, and flows past Bingley. By the time it joins the Ouse and decants into the Humber Estuary, it has been one of the hardest worked watercourses in Yorkshire. When the textile trades were at their height, the Aire was both a source of power for the woollen mills and a convenient dumping ground for industrial waste. But, like so many other West Yorkshire rivers, the water quality is now greatly improved.

Exploring St Ives
For part of this walk, you will be exploring the St Ives Estate, which from 1636 was owned by one of Bingley's most prominent families, the Ferrands. It was William Ferrand who, during the 1850s, landscaped the estate and created many of the paths and tracks that climb steeply through the woods. The view from the top of the hill is ample reward for your efforts. From the gritstone outcrop known as the Druid's Altar, you have a splendid panorama across Bingley and the Aire Valley. There is an inscription on Lady Blantyre's Rock, passed later on the walk, which commemorates William Ferrand's mother-in-law. Lady Blantyre often used to sit in the shade of this rock and read a book.

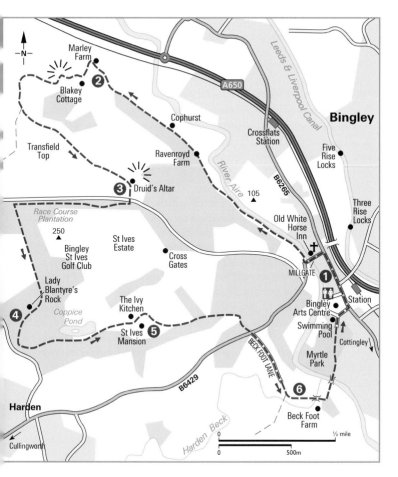

1. Walk northwest from the centre of Bingley towards the church. Go left at the traffic lights beside the Old White Horse pub into Millgate. Cross the River Aire and take the first right, Ireland Street. Swing immediately right again and then left along a riverside track, soon leaving the town behind. Reaching Ravenroyd Farm, bear right and pass between farm buildings to continue on a walled track to Cophurst. Pass left of the cottage and continue beside a wood at the edge of successive pastures.

2. A developing track leaves the third pasture through a gap. Continue to a stile and gate and skirt a hillock, eventually leaving over a stile by Marley Farm. Follow the rough track up left, passing Marley Brow. Where the track subsequently swings into a farm, bear off right on a grass trail across a bracken and scrub slope, ultimately winding up to a small gate. A narrow path rises through more trees. Keep right and then left at successive forks, shortly joining a wall on the right bounding the top of the wood. Eventually, after crossing a broad track, the path leads to a rocky outcrop known as the Druid's Altar, a striking viewpoint.

3. Bear right, after the rocks, to come to a meeting of tracks. Go through a gap in the wall opposite, onto a walled track into the St Ives Estate. Leave immediately through a kissing gate on the right onto a path that runs pleasantly for half a mile (800m) within Race Course Plantation. Ignoring the kissing gate leading out at the end, go left, now descending, initially still within trees through a golf course and then at the edge of open heather moor. When the accompanying wall later turns away, bear right with the main path, dropping through wood once more to come upon Lady Blantyre's Rock.

4. Descend with the main path, past exuberant displays of rhododendrons, and on beside Coppice Pond. Meeting a metalled drive, bear left, soon passing The Ivy Kitchen, the golf clubhouse and then, set back on the right, the house itself, St Ives Mansion.

5. Beyond the house, curve right and left to follow the main drive downhill for 0.5 miles (800m). Just after passing a car park, take a path left into woodland. Keep right where it immediately forks, to reach the B6429, the Bingley–Cullingworth road. Cross it and continue downhill on narrow Beck Foot Lane. After houses the lane becomes an unmade track leading down to a delectable spot: here you will find Beck Foot Farm, in a wooded setting by Harden Beck, with a ford and a packhorse bridge that dates back to 1723.

6. Cross the bridge to Beck Foot Farm and bear left past allotments. Where they end, take a path left to a footbridge over the River Aire. Walk ahead through Myrtle Park, leaving at its far side between the swimming pool and the supermarket on Myrtle Grove. Turn right and then left to return to the main road running through the town. The Old White Horse, past which the walk began, lies to the left.

Where to eat and drink

With 12th-century origins, the Old White Horse Inn is Bingley's oldest pub and housed the court, police cells and gibbet. Serving food at weekends, it has oodles of character, and claims several resident ghosts. On the St Ives estate, try The Ivy Kitchen.

What to see

Having been removed from the main street, Bingley's ancient stocks, butter cross and old market hall were re-sited in front of the Bingley Arts Centre, near the Market Square Tavern.

While you're there

Next to Bingley is the little town of Cottingley where, in 1917, two young girls took photographs of fairies by Cottingley Beck. Despite the fairies looking like paper cut-outs, the pictures were 'authenticated' by Arthur Conan Doyle, creator of the fiercely logical Sherlock Holmes. Pay a visit to Cottingley Beck, and listen out for the beating of tiny wings.

MOORLAND AROUND LAYCOCK AND GOOSE EYE

DISTANCE/TIME	8 miles (12.9km) / 3hrs 15min
ASCENT/GRADIENT	1,617ft (492m) / ▲ ▲
PATHS	Good paths and tracks, though can be muddy, take care with route finding, several stiles
LANDSCAPE	Wooded valley and heather moorland
SUGGESTED MAP	OS Explorer OL21 South Pennines
START/FINISH	Grid reference: SE032410
DOG FRIENDLINESS	On leads where sheep graze on sections of moorland
PARKING	In Laycock; roadside parking at Keighley end of village, close to village hall
PUBLIC TOILETS	None on route

To the west of Keighley, a tranche of moorland sits astride the border between Yorkshire and Lancashire. Here you can walk for miles without seeing another hiker – and perhaps with just curlew and grouse for company.

Unexpected mills

When we think of textile mills, we tend to associate them with cramped towns full of smoking chimneys. But the earliest mills were sited in surprisingly rural locations, often in the little steep-sided valleys known as cloughs where fast-flowing becks and rivers could be dammed and diverted to turn the waterwheels. There are reminders, in wooded Newsholme Dean, that even a watercourse as small as Dean Beck could be harnessed to provide power to a cotton mill in Goose Eye. Weirs along the beck helped to maintain a good head of water, and continue to be useful to locals – one of the mill dams is now popular with anglers.

Laycock and Goose Eye

The village of Laycock contains a number of handsome old houses in the typical South Pennine style. While Laycock sits on the hillside, with good valley views, neighbouring Goose Eye nestles in a hollow. The village was originally called 'Goose Heights', which the local dialect contracted to 'Goose Ay', and thence to the name we know today. Lovers of real ale will already be familiar with the name, as this was the home of the Goose Eye Brewery now based in Bingley.

A local museum

If you head to Keighley, Cliffe Castle Museum is worth a visit. Set in an attractive hillside park on Spring Gardens Lane in Keighley, it was built in the 1880s as a mansion for a wealthy mill owner, and its opulent halls were the scene of many prestigious parties. It is now Keighley's town museum, specialising in natural history and geology.

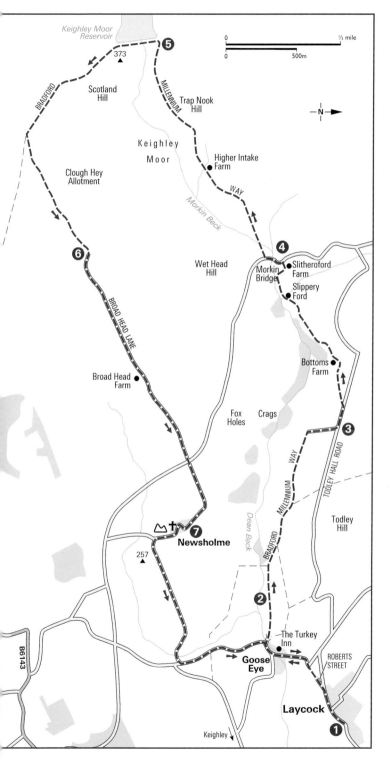

Keighley Moor
Reservoir

5

373

BRADFORD

Scotland
Hill

MILLENNIUM

Trap Nook
Hill

Keighley
Moor

Higher Intake
Farm

Clough Hey
Allotment

WAY

Morkin Beck

6

Wet Head
Hill

4

Morkin
Bridge

Slitheroford
Farm

Slippery
Ford

BROAD HEAD LANE

Broad Head
Farm

Bottoms
Farm

Fox
Holes

Crags

3

MILLENNIUM WAY

TODLEY HALL ROAD

Dean Beck

Todley
Hill

Newsholme

257

7

2

The Turkey
Inn

Goose
Eye

ROBERTS
STREET

B6143

Laycock

1

Keighley

0 ½ mile
0 500m

—N—▶

1. Walk through the village of Laycock. Where the road narrows, go left down a paved track, Roberts Street. Beyond terraced houses, descend along a narrow walled path to emerge onto a road, which you follow down into Goose Eye. Pass The Turkey Inn. Just 50yds (46m) after you cross Dean Beck, take the steps on your right and re-cross the beck on a footbridge. Follow the beck upstream and take a footbridge on the right, across the channel of a now-dry mill leat.

2. Carry on up the wooded valley, later passing through a gap in a wall. Ignore a path off right and keep ahead, breaking out onto a more open hillside. Before long, the way passes behind a farmhouse to join a farm track. Go left but then branch right on a rough track signed to Slippery Ford. Carry on through a gate, later fording a stream. Just beyond, fork right on a rising hollow path, which later develops as a track. Eventually swinging right it climbs to meet a lane.

3. Walk left along the road for 75yds (69m) before taking an access track on the left to Bottoms Farm. Entering the yard, waymarks indicate a small gate to the right. Skirt beside a barn to a stile from which a path to the left continues across the hillside. Through a gate, carry on over stiles across several fields. At the far side of the fourth field, drop left to find a confluence of two streams. Ford the side beck to a gate and carry on at the edge of another field above the main stream. At the field corner, turn up beside the wall, climbing to a gate near the top of the rise beside Slitheroford Farm. Walk through the yard and out to a lane. Follow the road down to the left to the beck at Morkin Bridge.

4. Reaching Morkin Bridge, turn off right to follow a metalled track through a gate. It rises steadily onto the moors above the fold of Morkin Beck, passing the lonely farm of Higher Intake and eventually leading to Keighley Moor Reservoir, the highest point on the walk.

5. Walk left, across the top of the dam. At the far end, ignore the signed track to the right and instead bear left at a concrete post along a gently descending moorland track. At a boggy section keep ahead, the vague path eventually becoming more distinct as it joins a wall. Follow it for 150yds (137m) to a gateway, turn through and then bear half right to cross a line of grouse butts (shooting stations) on a distinct but narrow path through the heather. Eventually, on meeting a track, follow it right over a cattle grid.

6. Soon leaving the moorland behind, Broad Head Lane runs straight for three-quarters of a mile (1.2km). Meeting a road by a farm, cross to a track opposite and follow it to cottages at Newsholme.

7. Wind forward between the houses and follow a lane downhill. After 250yds (229m), opposite the entrance to Green End Farm, turn left. Degrading to a track, the way eventually swings across a beck to meet a road. Follow it left down to Goose Eye and The Turkey Inn. Carry on steeply uphill to where the lane swings sharp left, branching off right to reverse your outward route up Roberts Street back to Laycock.

Where to eat and drink

The Turkey Inn, near the beginning of the walk in Goose Eye, is a splendid village pub with a reputation for good food.

THE PENDLE WAY FROM BARLEY

DISTANCE/TIME	5 miles (8km) / 2hrs 30min
ASCENT/GRADIENT	1,411ft (430m) / ▲ ▲ ▲
PATHS	Defined paths, lots of kissing gates, 1 stile
LANDSCAPE	Wooded valleys, moorland, hilltop views
SUGGESTED MAP	OS Explorer OL21 South Pennines
START/FINISH	Grid reference: SD823403
DOG FRIENDLINESS	On leads near livestock on moorland
PARKING	Pay-and-display car park in Barley
PUBLIC TOILETS	At car park

This walk begins in the village of Barley, which, in 1324, was known as Barelegh – meaning an infertile lea or meadow. It follows much of the route of the Pendle Way, signposted by a black witch flying on her broomstick across a yellow sky. You climb gently past the Lower Ogden Reservoir and the Upper Ogden Reservoir to the steep sided Ogden Clough, then strike off up Boar Clough, where the vegetation is indicative of acidic peat: ferns uncurl above bilberry shrubs, and verdant patches of moss and white bog cotton complete the patchwork. The going is soft on the peaty ground across Barley Moor to the summit of Pendle Hill. The descent down the Big End is steep but quick, followed by a lovely tree-lined walk beside a tiny beck to return to Barley.

Referred to as a sleeping lion, Pendle Hill slopes gently up the lion's back to fall away sharply down the face, known as the Big End. The summit affords a spectacular bird's-eye view over the Ribble Valley to Yorkshire's Three Peaks in the north and Lancashire's cotton towns of Padiham and Burnley nestling beneath the Pennine hills to the south. On the 1,827ft (557m) summit is the Beacon, a Bronze Age burial mound possibly 7,000 years old. It was Pendle Hill that George Fox climbed in 1652 and where he had his vision of enlightenment that led him to found the Quaker movement.

The name Pendle Hill means 'Hill Hill Hill'. If you lived below Pendle, you might well call it simply 'the Hill', and early Celtic inhabitants did just that – 'Pen'. Later incomers, not realising this, called it Pendle, meaning 'the hill called Pen'. This meaning too became obscured, and the name was later applied to the whole district.

Pendle witches

'Witch' comes from the Anglo-Saxon word 'wicca', meaning 'the wise ones' and were thought to possess magical powers. The Demdikes of Malkin Tower and the Chattox's of Higham were matriarchal families who lived in the Pendle area in the early 17th century. These self-confessed witches were accused of turning cattle into cats, turning the ale in the inn at Higham sour and bewitching the landlord's son to death, and paralysing a pedlar on the road to Colne. These were difficult times for independent women, witches or not, and 19 Pendle residents were eventually taken to the gaol at Lancaster Castle where they were charged with witchcraft. The Witch Trial took place in August 1612 and, after some dubious confessions, resulted in the execution by hanging of seven women and two men. The story has been fictionalised in many novels including Robert Neill's *Mist Over Pendle* (1951) and *The Familiars* (2019) by Stacey Halls.

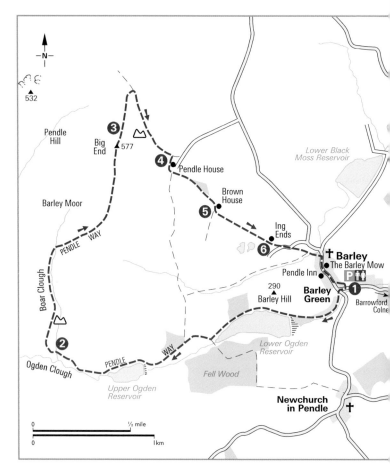

1. Exit the car park, turn right and cross the main road to a bridlepath that is signposted 'Ogden Clough', Pass the three-storey Barley Green farmhouse with its interesting row of corbels, proceed between circular gateposts, and pass a Water Works building on the right. Continue to a climb beside the grassy dam of the lower reservoir, where the metalled lane gives way to an unmade track. Continue straight ahead and join the Pendle Way as it leaves Fell Wood on the left; here you get your first clear view of Pendle Hill up to the right. Keep straight ahead to the bottom of the upper reservoir, cross a stile and ascend the track beside the dam. Follow the Pendle Way alongside the reservoir and

up Ogden Clough, passing through a kissing gate into open country. The path is obvious to another kissing gate, where the route bears right up a stony path that soon swings left and follows the contours.

2. Cross the stream in Boar Clough. An obvious, badly eroded, path climbs up to the right. Avoid the worst of this by continuing ahead a short distance, then climbing grassy slopes directly to a marker post. Either way is steep at first but soon gives way to a more gentle climb on soft ground along a cairn-marked route over Barley Moor to the summit trig point.

3. Walk along the summit escarpment to a wall with a ladder stile. Go right, staying this side of the wall, to a carved upright stone marking the Pendle Way; strike sharp right and descend steeply down the stone-stepped path.

4. Go right after the kissing gate at the bottom, signposted 'Barley', rounding the back of Pendle House to a yellow-topped post and bear left through another gate. Drop down the meadow, with a wall on the left, and through a gate at the bottom leading into another meadow. Keep on down to a kissing gate and walk through newly planted trees to another gate near a farm building. Turn right along a track as signposted, then bear left through the grounds of Brown House to join a tree-lined path between a stream and a wall.

5. Proceed through gates and over footbridges to reach a narrow cobbled lane. Exit onto a metalled road and turn left through the grounds of Ing Ends.

6. Soon after, cross a yellow waymarked footbridge on the right and bear left through a meadow and gates to pick up the stream on the left. On reaching the main road in Barley opposite the Primitive Methodist church, turn right through the village to a Pendle Way marker leading you off the road, through the playground and park to the car park beyond.

Where to eat and drink
Barley has a selection of places for refreshments. The Barley Mow restaurant offers good facilities. The Pendle Inn dates from 1930 and the fine, panelled interior is original. There's an open fire, good beer and food, available all day at weekends.

What to see
Pendle's thick blanket of peat supports significant types of flora including sedges, cranberry, crowberry, and if you're lucky, you might spot some cloudberry (sometimes known as mountain strawberry). Bearing fruit in June and July, look for the little orange clusters of berries. The moors of Pendle are more grassy, less dominated by heather than those of Bowland and there's a great variety of plants. Low-growing tormentil has yellow flowers like tiny Maltese crosses. The unmistakable fluffy white tufts of cotton grass, also known as bog cotton, are a marker of wet ground.

While you're there
Visit Wycoller Country Park, southeast of Colne, where the centrepiece is ruined Wycoller Hall, believed to be Ferndean Manor in Charlotte Brontë's *Jane Eyre*. It's a beautiful, atmospheric location – a remote upland valley that survived industrialisation and depopulation. There are waymarked walks, a picnic site, tea room and craft shop.

HAWORTH AND
THE BRONTË WAY

DISTANCE/TIME	8.1 miles (13km) / 3hrs 30min
ASCENT/GRADIENT	1,508ft (460m) / ▲▲
PATHS	Well signed and easy to follow
LANDSCAPE	Open moorland
SUGGESTED MAP	OS Explorer OL21 South Pennines
START/FINISH	Grid reference: SE029372
DOG FRIENDLINESS	On leads near sheep on open moorland
PARKING	Pay-and-display car park, near Brontë Parsonage
PUBLIC TOILETS	At entrance to car park

Who could have imagined, when the Revd Patrick Brontë became curate of the Church of St Michael and All Angels in 1820, that the little gritstone town of Haworth would become a literary hot spot to rival Grasmere and Stratford-upon-Avon? But visitors flock here in great numbers: some to gain some insights into the works of Charlotte, Emily and Anne, others just to enjoy a day out. If the shy sisters could see the Haworth of today, they would recognise the steep, cobbled main street. But they would no doubt be amazed to see the tourist industry that's built up to exploit their names and literary reputations. They would recognise the Georgian parsonage too. Now a museum, it has been painstakingly restored to reflect the lives of the Brontës and the rooms are filled with their personal treasures. That three such prodigious talents should be found within a single family is remarkable enough. To have created such towering works as *Jane Eyre* and *Wuthering Heights* while living in a bleakly inhospitable place is incredible. The public were unprepared for this trio of lady novelists, which is why all the books published during their lifetimes bore the androgynous pen names of Currer, Ellis and Acton Bell.

Literary tourism

After Patrick Brontë came to Haworth with his wife and six children, tragedy was never far away. His wife died the following year and two daughters did not live to adulthood. His only son, Branwell, succumbed to drink and drugs; Anne and Emily died aged 29 and 30 respectively. Only Charlotte lived long enough to marry but, after just one year of marriage, she, too, fell ill and died in 1855, aged 38. Revd Brontë survived them all, living to the ripe old age of 84.

Tourism is no recent development; by the middle of the 19th century, the first literary pilgrims were visiting Haworth. No matter how crowded this little town becomes, it is always possible to escape to the moors that surround it. You can follow, literally, in the footsteps of the three sisters as they sought freedom and inspiration, away from the stifling confines of the parsonage and the adjacent graveyard. As you explore these inhospitable moors, you'll get a greater insight into the literary world of the Brontës than those who stray no further than the souvenir shops and tea rooms of Haworth.

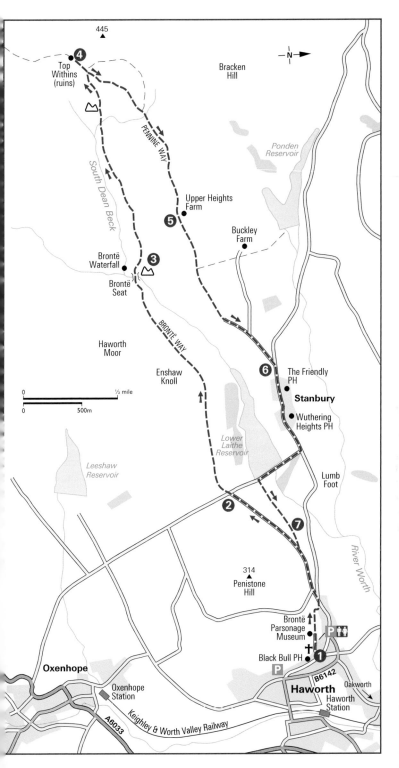

445 ▲

④ Top Withins (ruins)

Bracken Hill

PENNINE WAY

Ponden Reservoir

South Dean Beck

Upper Heights Farm ⑤

Buckley Farm

Brontë Waterfall
③
Brontë Seat

BRONTË WAY

Haworth Moor

Enshaw Knoll

⑥ The Friendly PH

Stanbury

Wuthering Heights PH

Lower Laithe Reservoir

0 ½ mile
0 500m

Leeshaw Reservoir

Lumb Foot

②

⑦

River Worth

314 ▲ Penistone Hill

Brontë Parsonage Museum

P 🚻

Black Bull PH

①

Oxenhope

P

B6142

Haworth

Oxenhope Station

Haworth Station

Oakworth

A6033

Keighley & Worth Valley Railway

N

1. Take the cobbled lane beside The King's Arms, signed to the Brontë Parsonage Museum. The lane soon becomes a paved field path that leads to the Haworth–Stanbury road. Walk left along the road and, after just 75yds (69m), take a left fork, signed to Penistone Hill. Continue along this quiet road to a T-junction.

2. Follow the track opposite, signed to the Brontë Waterfall. Becoming a path, it eventually descends to South Dean Beck where, close to the stone bridge, you will find the Brontë Seat (a boulder that resembles a chair) and the Brontë Waterfall. Cross the bridge and climb steeply uphill to a kissing gate and three-way sign.

3. Keep left, uphill, on a paved path signed 'Top Withins'. Beyond another kissing gate, ignore the later left fork. After dipping across a beck the path leads on, eventually climbing to a signpost by a ruined building. Walk a short distance left, uphill, to visit the ruin of Top Withins, which can be imagined as the inspiration for Emily Brontë's *Wuthering Heights*.

4. Retrace your steps to the signpost, but now keep ahead on a paved path, downhill, signed to Stanbury and Haworth and the Pennine Way. Follow a broad, clear track across the wide expanse of wild Pennine moorland. Carry on for a mile (1.6km) to Upper Heights Farm.

5. At a fork at the farm, bear left with the Pennine Way, shortly passing a second farm. Some 200yds (183m) further on at a junction, the Pennine Way leaves to the left. The route, however, continues with the track ahead signed to Stanbury and Haworth. As other tracks join, the way becomes metalled and leads to the main lane at the edge of Stanbury.

6. Bear right along the road through Stanbury, then take the first road on the right, signed to Oxenhope, and cross the dam of Lower Laithe Reservoir. Immediately beyond the dam, turn left onto a service road and fork right along an uphill track that meets the lane by Haworth Cemetery.

7. From here you retrace your outward route: walk left along the road, soon taking a gap stile on the right, to follow the paved field path back into Haworth.

Where to eat and drink
The Black Bull is Haworth's most famous public house, standing in the little cobbled square at the top of the steep main street. This is where Branwell Brontë came to drown his sorrows. These days you can also have a sandwich, or a snack, or perhaps choose something from the specials board.

While you're there
At the bottom of that famous cobbled street is Haworth Station, on the restored Keighley and Worth Valley Railway. Take a steam train journey on Britain's last remaining complete branch line railway, or browse through the books and railway souvenirs at the station shop.

OXENHOPE AND THE WORTH VALLEY RAILWAY

DISTANCE/TIME	6.75 miles (10.9km) / 3hrs
ASCENT/GRADIENT	1,360ft (415m) / ▲▲
PATHS	Good paths and tracks, many stiles
LANDSCAPE	Upland scenery, moor and pasture
SUGGESTED MAP	OS Explorer OL21 South Pennines
START/FINISH	Grid reference: SE032353
DOG FRIENDLINESS	Keep on leads along country lanes and near livestock
PARKING	Street parking in Oxenhope, near the Keighley and Worth Valley Railway station
PUBLIC TOILETS	None on route

Oxenhope is the terminus of the Keighley and Worth Valley Railway and also the last village in the Worth Valley. To the north are Haworth and Keighley; going south, into Calderdale and Hebden Bridge, requires you to gear down for a scenic drive over the lonely heights of Cock Hill. Apart from the railway, the village is best known for the Oxenhope Straw Race, held each year on the first Sunday in July. Competitors have to carry a bale of straw all around the village, while drinking as much beer as possible. Whoever finishes this assault course first is the winner, but it is the local charities that benefit most.

Keighley and Worth Valley Railway

The Keighley and Worth Valley line, running for 5 miles (8km) from Keighley to Oxenhope, is one of the longest established private railways in the country, and the last remaining complete branch line. It was built in 1867, when the trains were run by the Midland Railway to link to the main Leeds–Skipton line at Keighley. When the line was threatened with closure in 1962, local rail enthusiasts formed a preservation society which bought and restored the line and its stations. Ingrow station, for example, had been so badly vandalised that a complete station was 'trainsported' to the site stone by stone from Foulridge in Lancashire. Built to the typical Midland style, it now blends in well with the other stations on the line. A regular timetable has continued since 1968. Steam trains run every weekend throughout the year, and daily in summer. But the line doesn't just cater for tourists; locals in the Worth Valley appreciate the diesel services into Keighley which operate on almost 200 days per year.

The line runs through the heart of Brontë country, with stations at Oxenhope, Haworth, Oakworth, Danems, Ingrow and Keighley. The stations are a particular delight: fully restored, gas-lit and redolent of the age of steam. So when Edith Nesbitt's classic children's novel, *The Railway Children*, was being filmed in 1970, the Keighley and Worth Valley Railway was a natural choice of setting. Everyone who has seen the film (it's the one with Jenny Agutter) will enjoy revisiting this much-loved location.

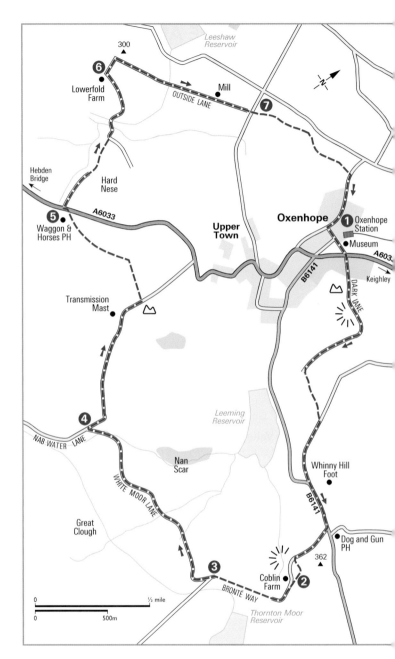

1. Begin along the minor lane beside the entrance of Oxenhope Station, which rises past the overflow car park to the A6033. Cross to Dark Lane opposite and climb steeply away. Later degrading to a track, it eventually ends at a lane. Go right down to the Denholme road (B6141) and follow it left to the Dog and Gun. Turn right opposite the pub into Sawood Lane.

2. At Coblin Farm, your route becomes a rough track. Through a gate at the end, join a metalled track and go right, which is signed 'Brontë Way'. Keep ahead past the entrance to Thornton Moor Reservoir, passing through a field gate along an unmade track. Ignore the Brontë Way, which then shortly drops off to the right.

3. At a fork 50yds (46m) further on, bear right before a gate on a descending track by the wall. It meanders for a mile (1.6km), passing a clump of trees and then crossing a watercourse before eventually meeting a moorland lane.

4. Go right here, eventually passing a cattle grid and a transmission mast. Carry on for another 150yds (137m) but, as the road begins a steep descent, take a wall stile on the left. Later, through another wall stile, head left, uphill, on a broad, walled track that leads to the Waggon and Horses pub.

5. Walk to the left, leaving after 30yds (27m) by a signpost on the right to a steeply descending track. Levelling after 300yds (274m), it swings right. Cross a stile by a gate on the left. Slant right down a couple of fields and continue the line across rough ground, dropping to a walled path at the bottom. Go left across a stream and climb away to Lowerfold Farm.

6. Walk forward past a row of cottages and go right on a metalled track. Follow it away down the hill above the Leeshaw Reservoir for 0.75 miles (1.2km). After passing a converted mill, it finally leads out to a lane.

7. Cross the lane and take the track ahead (signed to Marsh). Pass right of the end house, on a narrow walled path and continue across a small field. Through a courtyard, go left and right past cottages. Emerging, take the kissing gate opposite, from which a path runs through to a walled track. To the right, it leads past houses, across a field and out past more houses to a road. Go right back down into Oxenhope.

Where to eat and drink

The Waggon and Horses is at the walk's halfway point, on the Hebden Bridge Road out of Oxenhope. It enjoys great views over the valley and has a reputation for good food. If you take the train, there's an excellent café at Oxenhope Station in a stationary British Rail buffet car. It's open whenever trains are running and, additionally, on Wednesday to Sunday.

What to see

Visiting Oxenhope Station is like going back a hundred years. It has been lovingly restored, with enough period detail to make steam buffs dewy eyed with nostalgia. Take a trip to Haworth and back on the Keighley and Worth Valley Railway. You can return on foot along the Worth Way.

HARDCASTLE CRAGS AND CRIMSWORTH DEAN

DISTANCE/TIME	5 miles (8km) / 2hrs 30min
ASCENT/GRADIENT	1,359ft (414m) / ▲ ▲
PATHS	Good paths and tracks, plus open pasture
LANDSCAPE	Woodland, fields and moorland fringe
SUGGESTED MAP	OS Explorer OL21 South Pennines
START/FINISH	Grid reference: SD987293
DOG FRIENDLINESS	Keep dogs on leads near livestock
PARKING	National Trust pay-and-display car parks at Midgehole, near Hebden Bridge (accessible via A6033, Keighley Road)
PUBLIC TOILETS	Just before car parks at Midgehold

Hebden Bridge, just 4 miles (6.4km) from the Yorkshire/Lancashire border, has been a popular place to visit ever since the railway was extended across the Pennines, through the Calder Valley. But those train passengers weren't coming for a day out in a grimy little mill town; the big attraction was the wooded valley of Hebden Dale – usually called 'Hardcastle Crags' – just a short charabanc ride away. Here were shady woods, easy riverside walks and places to spread out a picnic blanket. To people who lived in the terraced streets of Bradford, Leeds or Halifax, Hardcastle Crags must have seemed idyllic. The steepsided valley became known as 'Little Switzerland' – at least to the writers of tourist brochures. The only disappointment, in fact, was the crags themselves: unassuming gritstone outcrops, almost hidden by trees.

Industrial demands

The Industrial Revolution created a huge demand for water: for mills, factories and domestic use. To quench the thirst of the rapidly expanding textile towns, many steep-sided valleys, known in the South Pennines as cloughs, were dammed to create reservoirs. Six of these lie within easy walking distance of Hardcastle Crags. They represented huge feats of civil engineering by the hundreds of navvies who built them, around the end of the 19th century, with picks and shovels. The men were housed in a shanty town, known as Dawson City, and both men and materials were transported to the work sites by a convoluted steam-powered railway system that crossed the valley on an elaborate wooden viaduct. Hardcastle Crags escaped the indignity of being turned into a reservoir, but three times during the last 60 years (the last time was in 1970) plans were drawn up to flood the valley. And three times, thankfully, wiser counsels prevailed and the plans were turned down.

Lord Savile, a major landowner in the area, once owned the valley. It was he who supplemented the natural woodland with plantings of new trees, particularly pines, and laid out the walks and the carriage drive. In 1948 he donated Hardcastle Crags, and the nearby valley of Crimsworth Dean, to the

National Trust, so now the future of this delightful valley looks secure and local people will be able to continue to enjoy this valuable amenity.

Hardcastle Crags are a haven for wildlife. Birders can look out for pied flycatchers, woodpeckers, jays, sparrowhawks and the ubiquitous dipper – which never strays from the environs of Hebden Water. In spring there are displays of bluebells; in summer the woods are filled with birdsong; the beech woods are a riot of colour as the leaves turn each autumn.

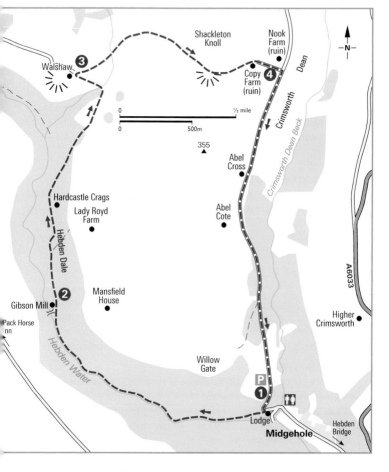

1. From the car park at Midgehole, walk back to the main drive. Go left towards the lodge but, just past the information board, immediately double back right on a path falling to a picnic area beside the river. Keep left whenever there is a choice of paths and continue upstream for a mile (1.6km) to reach Gibson Mill, occasionally climbing above the river where it becomes constricted between rocky banks.

2. Joining the main drive, follow it left beyond the mill, soon passing the crags that give the woods their name. Keep right at a later fork, shortly emerging from the trees and the National Trust estate to join a rough metalled drive.

It runs left to the farm and adjacent cottages at Walshaw, which enjoy a terrific prospect along the Hebden Water valley.

3. Just before you reach the houses – when you are opposite some barns – turn sharp right through a gate onto an enclosed track (signed to Crimsworth Dean). Running on as a field track, it peters out beyond another gate to follow a wall over the shoulder of Shackleton Knoll. Approaching the watershed, the path slips through a gate to continue on the wall's opposite flank. Developing as a track, it later turns through another gate and drops into Crimsworth Dean, ending at a junction beside the ruin of Nook Farm. Running the length of the valley, the rough way is the old road from Hebden Bridge to Howarth and is a great walk to contemplate for another day.

4. For now, however, turn right along this elevated track, passing a farm on the left. You can make a short detour right at the next fork to see Abel Cross, actually a pair of old waymarker stones standing beside the track. Return to the main track and continue down the valley, soon re-entering the woodland of the National Trust estate. Keep left at successive forks, eventually returning to the car park at Midgehole.

Where to eat and drink
The Pack Horse Inn can be found on the unclassified road between Colden and Brierfield, just beyond the wooded valley of Hardcastle Crags. It is one of many solitary, exposed pubs to be found in Pennine Yorkshire, which existed to cater for the drovers and packhorse men. It remains a favourite with travellers, but is closed Mondays and Tuesdays.

What to see
Hebden Water rushes picturesquely through the wooded valley of Hardcastle Crags. These upland rivers and streams are the perfect habitat for an attractive little bird called the dipper. Dark brown, with a blaze of white on its breast, the dipper never strays from water. Unique among British birds, it has perfected the trick of walking underwater.

While you're there
Walk the old road from Hebden Bridge to Haworth (it's marked on the OS map) that includes the section of track through wooded Crimsworth Dean. The old road is never hard to find, and offers easy walking with terrific views all the way. Have lunch in Haworth, and take the easy way back to Hebden Bridge – by bus.

JUMBLE HOLE AND COLDEN CLOUGH

DISTANCE/TIME	6 miles (9.7km) / 3hrs
ASCENT/GRADIENT	1,831ft (558m) / ▲ ▲
PATHS	Good paths, many stiles
LANDSCAPE	Steep-sided valleys, fields and woodland
SUGGESTED MAP	OS Explorer OL21 South Pennines
START/FINISH	Grid reference: SD991271
DOG FRIENDLINESS	Keep on leads near livestock and roads
PARKING	Pay-and-display car parks in Hebden Bridge
PUBLIC TOILETS	Hebden Bridge and Townfield Lane, Heptonstall

This walk links the little town of Hebden Bridge with the old hand-weaving village of Heptonstall, using sections of a waymarked walk, the Calderdale Way. The hill village of Heptonstall was, in its time, an important centre of the textile trade and at the hub of a complex network of old trackways, mostly used by packhorse trains carrying wool and cotton. Heptonstall's Cloth Hall, where cloth was bought and sold, dates from the 16th century, when Hebden Bridge was little more than a river crossing on an old packhorse causeway.

Wheels of industry

Heptonstall prospered when textiles were still a cottage industry, with spinning and weaving undertaken in isolated farmhouses. As the processes became mechanised during the Industrial Revolution, communities sprang up wherever a ready supply of running water could turn waterwheels to drive the new machinery. Heptonstall was literally left high and dry and a new settlement grew down in the valley at the confluence of two fast-flowing rivers, the Calder and Hebden Water. There, large mills enabled the textile processes to be developed on an industrial scale. At one time there were more than 30 mills in Hebden Bridge, their chimneys belching thick smoke into the Calder Valley. It used to be said that the only time you could see the town from the surrounding hills was during Wakes Week, the mill-hands' traditional holiday.

With Hebden Bridge hemmed in by hills, and the mills occupying much of the available land on the valley bottom, the workers' houses had to be built up the steep slopes. An ingenious solution to the problem was to build 'top and bottom' houses, one dwelling on top of another – best viewed on the last leg of the walk. Today, Hebden Bridge has reinvented itself as the 'capital' of Upper Calderdale, a place to enjoy a day out. The town is known for its excellent walking country, Bohemian population, narrowboat trips along the Rochdale Canal and its popular summer arts festival.

Jumble Hole Clough is a typical South Pennine steep-sided, wooded valley. Though a tranquil scene today, this little valley was once a centre of industry, with four mills exploiting the fast-flowing beck descending to the River Calder. You can see remains of these mills, and some of their mill ponds, on this walk.

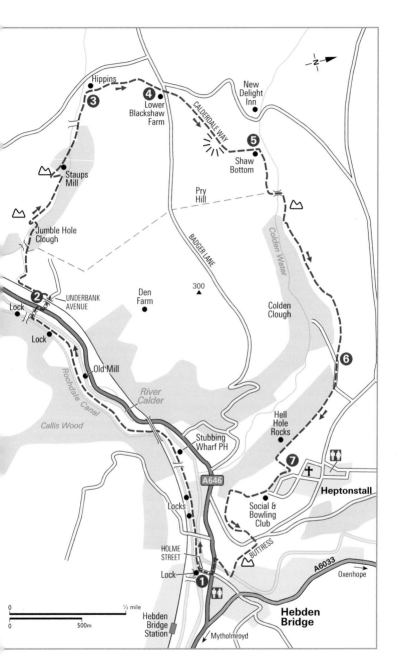

1. Begin along Holme Street, off the main A646 just east of the bridge, to the Rochdale Canal. Go right to follow the tow path beneath two bridges, past the Stubbing Wharf pub and beneath a railway bridge. Carry on for another 0.75 miles (1.2km) before turning off before the next bridge to follow a track to reach the A646.

2. Cross the road and turn right for 75yds (69m) to take Underbank Avenue, on the left. Walk beneath the railway and go left again, past houses, to where another road comes through the viaduct. Go sharp right on a track past a mill, and follow the beck up into the woodland of Jumble Hole Clough. Where the track later swings sharp right, leave across a stone bridge onto a track rising steeply through a hairpin. Higher up as it wheels left, take the narrow path ahead to continue above the beck. Ignore a later intersecting path and climb beyond to a stile. Join another path down to Staups Mill. The climb resumes beside the ruin to reach a footbridge. Scale the opposite bank and go left in front of a signpost by a gap in a wall to come out at Hippins.

3. Join the Calderdale Way, turning right up a track between farm buildings to a stile. Follow a path to the next stile and on beside a wall. Cross a track at Apple Tree Farm and continue over a couple of stiles on a causeway to a row of cottages. Pass the end of the terrace, crossing more stiles and a rough pasture to a kissing gate. Follow the onward causeway to a farm, there following a track out to the lane at Blackshaw Head.

4. Cross to a small gate almost opposite and bear half right across the field to a stile, then follow the right edge of the next field. Continue on a diagonal line across successive fields, eventually reaching a walled track. Walk down to Shaw Bottom and bear left beside the house to a junction.

5. The New Delight Inn is to the left, but the route lies to the right, the way degrading to a stony track. After 200yds (183m), bear left beside a waypost on a stepped path dropping steeply to cross Colden Water. Take the rising path, but then keep right higher up to follow a stone causeway along the valley side above the trees. Carry on as you later break out into a field. Over a stile at the far corner, ignore the adjacent gate and swing around the wall corner to pick up the continuing flagged path. Eventually meeting a rising track, go left to a junction and turn right on a tarmac drive. Bear off left behind a cottage, the causeway resuming over a stile beyond. Shortly meeting an intersecting track, go right and follow it out to a lane.

6. Walk up the hill, leaving just before a bend through a gap in the right-hand wall. From here your path meanders through woodland (it's a bit of a scramble in places). Emerging from the trees, continue above the edge to Hell Hole Rocks. Turn away from the viewpoint along a walled path between gardens. Cross a street to the ongoing path, which shortly meets a track behind houses.

7. Go right, emerging opposite the Social and Bowling Club. Turn right on a contained path. As the ground falls away, curve left by the boundary, eventually dropping through a wall onto a crossing path. Walk left to meet a track and go right to a junction. Bear left along the lower, main road, doubling sharply right after 50yds (46m) onto the Buttress, an old packhorse trail that drops steeply back to Hebden Bridge.

Where to eat and drink

As you'd expect, Hebden Bridge is full of walker-and-dog-friendly pubs, cafés and restaurants.

THE BRIDESTONE ROCKS FROM LYDGATE

DISTANCE/TIME	6.25 miles (10.1km) / 3hrs
ASCENT/GRADIENT	1,615ft (492m) / ▲ ▲
PATHS	Moorland and packhorse paths, some quiet roads, several stiles
LANDSCAPE	Steep-sided valley and open moorland
SUGGESTED MAP	OS Explorer OL21 South Pennines
START/FINISH	Grid reference: SD923255
DOG FRIENDLINESS	Keep on leads along lanes and near grazing sheep
PARKING	Roadside parking in Lydgate, 1.5 miles (2.4km) out of Todmorden, on A646, signposted to Burnley
PUBLIC TOILETS	None on route

The Long Causeway, between Halifax and Burnley, is an ancient trading route, possibly dating back to the Bronze Age. Crosses and waymarker stones helped to guide travellers across the moorland wastes, though most of them have been lost or damaged in the intervening years. Amazingly, Mount Cross has survived intact: a splendid, though crudely carved, example of the Celtic 'wheel-head' design. Opinions differ about its age but it is certainly the oldest human artefact in the area, erected at least 1,000 years ago.

The Bridestones

The hills and moors to the north of Todmorden are dotted with gritstone outcrops. The impressive piles of Orchan Rocks and Whirlaw Stones are both encountered on this walk. But the most intriguing rock formations are to be found at the Bridestones. One rock in particular has been weathered by wind and water into a teardrop shape, and stands on a base that looks far too slender to support its great weight.

Wind and water power

Further along the edge to the northwest, and well placed to catch the winds funnelled along the valley, are the tall turbines of Coal Clough Windfarm. With a capacity of around 9.6 megawatts, enough to power around 5,500 homes, it was opened in 1992 and was one of the first such schemes to be commissioned in this country.

The Cliviger Valley links two towns – Todmorden in West Yorkshire and Burnley in Lancashire – that expanded with the textile trade, and then suffered when that trade went into decline. The valley itself is narrow and steep-sided, in places almost a gorge. Into its cramped confines are shoehorned the road, railway line, the infant River Calder and communities such as Portsmouth, Cornholme and Lydgate that grew up around the textile mills. The mills were powered by fast-flowing becks, running off the steep hillsides. The valley is almost a microcosm of the Industrial Revolution: by no means beautiful, but full of character. This area is particularly well provided with good footpaths, some of them still paved with their original causeway stones.

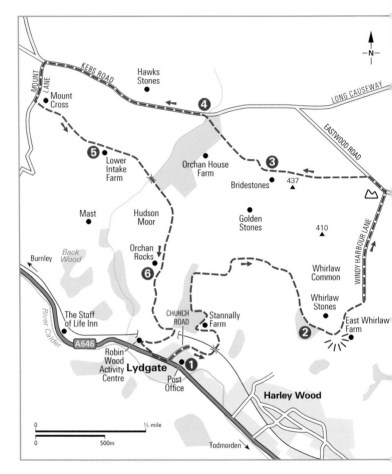

1. From the post office in Lydgate, take Church Road. At the end go right into Owlers Walk and continue along a contained path. Meeting a track at its end, follow it beneath a railway bridge and up to Stannally Farm. Walk past the buildings and swing right as the track zig-zags steeply up the wooded hillside. Eventually breaking out onto the edge of open moor it swings right towards a farm. Pass on the left of the farmhouse and then bear left up a narrower walled track. When you meet another walled track, go right towards a rocky outcrop on the first horizon. Beyond two gates, the path crosses onto the rough common that aprons Whirlaw Stones.

2. A causeway path skirts the base of the outcrop, giving panoramic views of the Cliviger Valley, Todmorden and Stoodley Pike. Keep going through gates until you reach a junction above East Whirlaw Farm. There turn sharp left along a stony track that winds up beside the outcrop to meet the end of Windy

Harbour Lane. Carry on up the lane, which shortly leads to Eastwood Road. Go left for just 150yds (137m). Where the wall ends, take a kissing gate on the left. A grassy path leads you to another fascinating collection of rocks, known as the Bridestones.

3. Continue past the Bridestones across a landscape of scattered boulders. Keep ahead, dropping to cross a ruined wall. Continue ahead past wayposts, the path curving above the edge and eventually falling to a gate and stile. Follow a track right out to a lane.

4. Go left, along the road for 0.75 miles (1.2km), passing below the Hawks Stones on the right and a handful of houses, until you come to a minor road on the left. This is Mount Lane, signed to Shore. Walk down for 300yds (274m) before turning left onto a broad bridleway. Look out for Mount Cross, which stands a short way along, over the wall in a field to your left.

5. Bear left past Lower Intake Farm on a path that soon resumes as a track. Cross an intersecting track and, later, a bridge spanning a stream before reaching a stile, 250yds (229m) further along on the right. Ignore the stile, but take the adjacent track, which drops alongside a wall past another gritstone outcrop, Orchan Rocks.

6. Where the wall bears left, beyond the rocks, follow it downhill to a stile. You now join a farm track that makes a serpentine descent through woodland back to Lydgate. Reaching the former Board School, now the Robin Wood Activity Centre, turn sharp left back to the main road.

Where to eat and drink

The Staff of Life Inn on the main A646 at Lydgate below Eagle's Crag is a cosy real ale pub offering a warm welcome to walkers. The bar has rotating guest beers and locally produced organic beers as well as a range of ciders. The food is all home-made, using fresh, organic and local produce wherever possible.

What to see

In geological terms, the South Pennines are largely made up of millstone grit and coarse sandstone. Where the gritstone is visible, it forms rocky crags and outcrops, like those encountered on this walk. The typical landscape is moorland of heather and peat, driven by steep-sided valleys. Here, in the confines of the steep Cliviger Valley, road, rail and river cross and re-cross each other – like the flex of an old-fashioned telephone.

While you're there

If you continue along the Long Causeway, you'll soon come to Coal Clough Windfarm. These huge wind turbines can be found on the crest of many South Pennine hills, attracting strong winds and equally strong opinions. To some people they represent a sustainable future for energy, to others they are ugly intrusions on the landscape.

ALONG LANGFIELD EDGE TO STOODLEY PIKE

DISTANCE/TIME	9 miles (14.5km) / 4hrs
ASCENT/GRADIENT	1,821ft (555m) / ▲ ▲
PATHS	Good paths and tracks, several stiles
LANDSCAPE	Open moorland
SUGGESTED MAP	OS Explorer OL21 South Pennines
START/FINISH	Grid reference: SD936241
DOG FRIENDLINESS	On leads as sheep grazing throughout
PARKING	Car parks in centre of Todmorden
PUBLIC TOILETS	Brook Street, Todmorden

Todmorden – call it 'Tod' if you want to sound like a local – is a border town, standing at the junction of three valley routes. Before the town was included in the old West Riding, the Yorkshire–Lancashire border divided the town in two. Todmorden's splendid town hall, built in an unrestrained classical Greek style, reflects this dual personality. On top of the town hall are carved figures which represent, on one side, the Lancashire cotton trade, and, on the other side, Yorkshire agriculture and engineering.

Stoodley Pike

Stoodley Pike is a ubiquitous sight around the Calder Valley, an unmistakable landmark. It seems you only need to turn a corner, or crest a hill, and it appears on the horizon. West Yorkshire is full of monuments built on prominent outcrops, but few of them dominate the view in quite the way that Stoodley Pike does.

In 1814, a trio of patriotic Todmorden men convened in a local pub, the Golden Lion. Now that the Napoleonic War was over, they wanted to commemorate the peace with a suitably grand monument. So they organised a public subscription, and raised enough money to erect a monument, 1,476ft (450m) up on Langfield Edge, overlooking the town. Construction was halted, briefly, when Napoleon rallied his troops, and was not completed until the following year, when he was finally defeated at the Battle of Waterloo.

This original monument was undone by the Pennine weather. Ironically, it collapsed in 1854, on the very day that the Crimean War broke out. Another group of local worthies came together (yes, at the Golden Lion again) to raise more money. So the Stoodley Pike we see today is Mark II: 131ft (40m) high and built to commemorate the ending of hostilities in the Crimea. It remains visible for almost every step of this exhilarating ridge walk. As well as being a favourite destination for local walkers, the Pike is visited by walkers on the Pennine Way.

Remember to pack a torch for this walk. By climbing a flight of unlit stone steps inside the monument, you emerge at a viewing platform offering wonderful panoramic views over Calderdale and beyond.

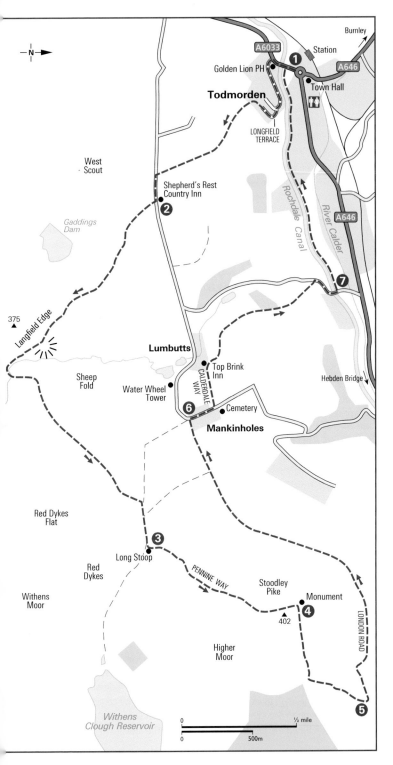

West
Scout

*Gaddings
Dam*

375
▲ Langfield Edge

Sheep
Fold

Red Dykes
Flat

Red
Dykes

Withens
Moor

*Withens
Clough Reservoir*

Burnley

A6033

Station

Golden Lion PH

A646

Town Hall

Todmorden

LONGFIELD
TERRACE

1

Shepherd's Rest
Country Inn

2

Rochdale Canal

River Calder

A646

7

Lumbutts

Top Brink
Inn

CALDERDALE WAY

Water Wheel
Tower

6

Cemetery

Hebden Bridge

Mankinholes

Long Stoop

3

PENNINE WAY

Stoodley
Pike

Monument

4

▲
402

Higher
Moor

LONDON ROAD

5

0 _____ ½ mile

0 _____ 500m

1. From the town hall in the centre of Todmorden, take the Rochdale road (A6033), cross the canal, turning left and immediately left again around the Golden Lion pub to walk up Longfield Road. Keep ahead as the main street veers away to new houses, but then swing right with Longfield Road up to Longfield Terrace at the end. Just before the row of houses, bear left on a track climbing between the fields behind. When the track forks, keep left to a farm, from where you will get the first glimpse of your destination – Stoodley Pike – on the horizon ahead. Continue along the farm track to a road. Go left, to find a pub, the Shepherd's Rest Country Inn, in splendid isolation.

2. Opposite the pub, take a track leading through a gate, uphill, onto Langfield Common. Keep ahead past a waymark along a distinct and well-graded path that rises across the steep hillside below Langfield Edge. Levelling at the top, it is joined by another path to round the head of the clough. The way runs on above the edge, eventually intersecting a broader path, the Pennine Way. Go left towards the distant monument.

3. Passing a stone seat, the path falls to a junction. Climb ahead past the leaning ancient waystone of Long Stoop. The way soon levels for the final stretch to the tower, 0.75 miles (1.2km) further on.

4. From the monument, swing right, walking down to a wall stile. After a few paces cross a second stile in the adjacent wall, from which the path drops more steeply to a lower track, London Road.

5. Follow the track left in a long and gentle descent to come out onto a lane. Go right, into the hamlet of Mankinholes.

6. After 0.25 miles (400m), opposite a cemetery and former Wesleyan Sunday school, turn off left along a walled path, signed the 'Pennine Bridleway'. It winds between fields to the Top Brink Inn at Lumbutts. Turn right between houses and continue at the field-edge along a causeway path. Passing through a squeeze gap into the third field, bear half right across the slope. Keep going beyond a broken wall, the path shortly closing beside a high fence. Meeting a farm track head downhill to emerge by cottages. Follow the lane right, swinging in front of a converted mill to a bridge spanning the Rochdale Canal.

7. Drop right to the tow path and follow the canal back under the bridge into the centre of Todmorden.

Where to eat and drink
The isolated Shepherd's Rest Country Inn is near the beginning of this walk, while the Top Brink Inn at Lumbutts is towards the end. Back in town, the Golden Lion serves Thai food and has regular live music, and Todmorden has plenty of other food outlet options.

What to see
London Road, the fancifully named track you follow from Stoodley Pike down into Mankinholes, was a 'cotton famine road'. When the cotton trade suffered a slump, mill owner John Fielden of Todmorden put some of his men to work on building this road, so he could ride his carriage up to Stoodley Pike. Fielden also built Dobroyd Castle, its castellated turrets on a hill overlooking the town.

HALIFAX AND THE SHIBDEN VALLEY

DISTANCE/TIME	5 miles (8km) / 2hrs 30min
ASCENT/GRADIENT	1,541ft (470m) / ▲ ▲
PATHS	Old packhorse tracks and field paths
LANDSCAPE	Surprisingly rural, considering the proximity to Halifax
SUGGESTED MAP	OS Explorer 288 Bradford & Huddersfield
START/FINISH	Grid reference: SE096251
DOG FRIENDLINESS	Keep on leads crossing busy roads
PARKING	Choice of pay-and-display car parks in Halifax
PUBLIC TOILETS	At Shibden Park

Set among the Pennine hills, Halifax was a town in the vanguard of the Industrial Revolution. Its splendid civic buildings and huge mills are an indication of the town's prosperity, won from the woollen trade. Ironically, the most splendid building of all came close to being demolished. The Piece Hall, built in 1779, predates the industrial era. Here, in a total of 315 rooms on three colonnaded floors, the hand-weavers of the district would offer their wares (known as 'pieces') for sale to cloth merchants. The colonnades surround a massive square. The mechanisation of the weaving process left the Piece Hall largely redundant. In the intervening years it has served a variety of purposes, including as a venue for political oration and as a wholesale market. During the 1970s, having narrowly escaped the wrecking ball, it was spruced up and given a new lease of life. It now houses a visitor centre, art gallery and speciality shops and hosts a programme of events throughout the year.

The Magna Via

The cobbled thoroughfare up Beacon Hill is known as the Magna Via. Until 1741, when a turnpike road was built, this was the only possible approach to Halifax from the east, for both foot and packhorse traffic. Also known as Wakefield Gate, the Magna Via linked up with the Long Causeway, the old high level road to Burnley. That intrepid 18th-century traveller, Daniel Defoe, was one of those who struggled up this hill. 'We quitted Halifax not without some astonishment at its situation, being so surrounded with hills, and those so high as makes the coming in and going out of it exceedingly troublesome'. The route was superseded in the 1820s by the turnpike constructed through Godley Cutting. Today the Magna Via, too steep for modern motor vehicles, remains a fascinating relic of the past.

Shibden Hall

Situated on a hill above Halifax, this magnificent half-timbered house is set in 90 acres (36ha) of beautiful, rolling parkland. Dating from 1420, the hall has been owned by prominent local families – the Oates, Saviles, Waterhouses and, latterly, the Listers. All these families left their mark, but the core of the original house remains intact. The rooms are furnished in period style, to show how they might have looked over almost six centuries. The oak furniture and panelling have that patina of age that antique forgers try in vain to emulate. Barns and other outbuildings have been converted into a folk museum, with displays of old vehicles, tools and farm machinery. Shiden Hall was home to landowner and diarist Anne Lister, who's life is explored in the BBC drama *Gentleman Jack*.

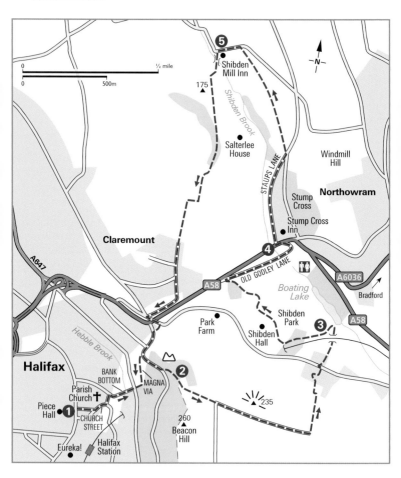

1. Begin opposite the tall spire that once belonged to Square Church, walking down Alfred Street East and left along Church Street, passing the smoke-blackened parish church. Bear left again into Lower Kirkgate, then right along Bank Bottom. Cross Hebble Brook and walk uphill; where the road bears sharp left, keep straight ahead up a steep cobbled lane, the Magna Via. Meeting a road at the top, go right for about 200yds (183m). Just after the entrance to a warehouse, take a cobbled path on the left that makes a steep ascent up Beacon Hill.

2. Keep with the main trail, which, higher up, curves left over the shoulder of the hill and runs beneath a high buttress wall to a kissing gate and barrier. Walk forward along a broad cinder track, taking the left fork a little further on where views open across the surprisingly rural Shibden Valley. After a further 100yds (91m), take a walled path on the left. Drop steeply to a small housing estate and turn right out to the main road. Almost opposite, beside a farm entrance, a path continues downhill, passing beneath the railway line into Shibden Park.

3. Walk forward to the lake and bear left past the boathouse up to a junction with the main drive. Go left and then left again in front of a pool onto a track that climbs beside the railway embankment. Reaching another pool, the house and gardens are to the left, otherwise, branch right towards the car park. At the next junction, drop right past a display of traditional walling, descending through trees to a drive. Climb left to the park entrance and turn right down Old Godley Lane. It finally swings left up to the main road at Stump Cross.

4. Cross over the road and take Staups Lane, to the left of Stump Cross Inn. Walk along the lane, which soon becomes cobbled, to meet another road at the top. Go left and immediately left again down a drive, which, through a gate, continues across the fields into Shibden Dale. Emerging at the far end onto a lane, turn left down to the Shibden Mill Inn.

5. Swing left past the pub, leaving the far end of the car park on a track across Shibden Brook. At a fork, bear right, later passing an isolated house. Beyond, a narrower path winds up to Claremount. Keep ahead along a street that ultimately bends right above Godley Cutting. At the end, go left over a bridge spanning the main road and then immediately descend steps on the right to a street below. Go left to its end and then right to retrace your outward route into Halifax.

Where to eat and drink

At the halfway point of this walk is Shibden Mill Inn. Tucked away in a leafy corner of Shibden Dale, yet close to the centre of Halifax, this picturesque inn enjoys the best of both worlds. A sympathetic reworking of an old mill, this is the place for good food and, when the weather is kind, a drink in the beer garden.

What to see

The bird's-eye view of Halifax from Beacon Hill is well worth the effort of climbing it. A century ago this view would have looked very different: most people's idea of William Blake's 'dark satanic mills' were here in unhealthy profusion, casting a dense pall of sulphurous smoke over the valley.

While you're there

As well as the Piece Hall, which houses an art gallery and craft shops, children will enjoy a visit to visit Eureka!, a hands-on discovery museum. It is designed for children up to the age of 12, with more than 400 interactive exhibits exploring science, nature and the world.

NOTES

NOTES

NOTES

Discover quality and friendly B&Bs

RatedTrips.com

AA